ANGI ...iANAGEMENT

UNDERSTANDING. HEALING. FREEDOM.

JOHN CRAWFORD

First Published: June 2016 as "You Can Fix Your Anger – Temper Management In An Unsympathetic World/Cool It" Re-titled August 2017

www.youcanfixyouranxiety.com

Re-Published: April 2017

ISBN-13:978-1975731465

ISBN-10:1975731468

Shadow cannot exist without light.

The "Yin/Yang" Symbol represents the duality in life – light and dark, good and evil, strong and weak, fire and water, expanding/contracting, angry or calm. The dot inside each section acknowledges that each force contains a measure of the other. Opposites therefore are not merely opposed to each other. They are also complementary.

FREE BOOK OFFER

As a valued reader, I'd like to invite you to join me by becoming a member of my free reader's group and download my third book "Dear Anxiety: This Is My Life" PLUS two professionally recorded relaxation recordings delivering authentic hypnosis experiences for beating stress!   All **absolutely free of charge.** No strings. Just sign up with your email address and you'll be added to the group, and kept in the loop! You can unsubscribe at any time!

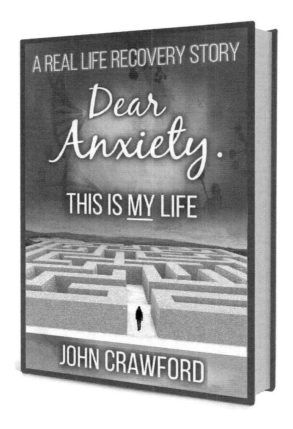

Here's the link:-

https://goo.gl/A3MQoi

OR just visit www.youcanfixyouranxiety.com

DISCLAIMER

I am a fully-qualified experienced hypno/psychotherapist. I am not a medically trained Doctor or Psychiatrist. I have taken every care to ensure that the information presented in this book is both ethical and responsible, and the information and techniques within this book have been safely used with my clients during my career.

However, if you have been diagnosed with, or believe you may be suffering from any form of psychiatric condition, you should seek professional help, and you should not use this book without the consent and blessing of your qualified formal medical healthcare provider. To all readers, please ensure that you read, understand, and agree to the following disclaimer before proceeding:-

This book is provided on an "as is" basis. I cannot assess nor guarantee that this book is suitable for your needs, or for use by you. You use this book at your own risk. The information offered in this book is offered as complementary therapeutic information. Information and content offered throughout this book are not offered as medical treatment, or diagnosis of a medical condition, and no such suggestion may be implied by you or me. If you are suffering from any medical condition or believe that you may need medical or psychiatric treatment, you are advised to see your Doctor or formal healthcare provider. By your use of this book, no medical, advisory, therapeutic, or professional relationship is implied or established between you and myself. Any information provided in this book is for information purposes only and does not replace or amend your Doctor's advice. Any action you may take arising from your use of this book, or any of the exercises contained within, including the use of relaxation recording/s, is undertaken entirely at your own risk and discretion. If any of the exercises contained within this book make you feel uncomfortable or distressed in any way, you agree to discontinue using them immediately. Use of this book does not guarantee a cure of any mental, emotional, or medical condition, and no such suggestion may be implied. This book and the information contained within it have not been audited by any official bodies, either, professional, regulatory, or governmental.

How This Book Can Help You

It may come as a surprise to you to learn that anger is as much a stress-related problem as being clinically anxious or depressed. Here's the thing though. If you're clinically anxious or depressed, people are largely sympathetic, and rightly so. Being anxious and/or depressed is a pretty horrendous experience. But, it seems that we are culturally far less forthcoming with our understanding when it comes to anger. Instead, anger is often seen as a weakness of character. Somehow it's considered **your** fault that you're so angry. In the absence of any other explanation, it's quite normal for the "angry" person to go along with this assessment and end up feeling increasingly worthless and isolated. Anger Management is not as simple as "willing" yourself to stop being angry. We need specific understanding if we are to find our calm. Being unable to control your temper is no less of an illness than being anxious or depressed, and it deserves every bit as much sympathy.

This is not to condone terrible behaviour, nor is it an invitation to pity yourself. I am not taking the position of a "bleeding heart liberal" here. Anger and hate are responsible for the very worst atrocities in this World, and anyone determined to remain hateful, for whatever reason, won't be helped. Very sadly, there are people in this World who are bad to the bone. This book won't help someone like that, but that's not who it's for. My guess is that if you have taken the time to read to this point, then you're not one of those people!

I have been a professional therapist specialising in the treatment of stress-related disorders for the last thirteen years of my life. Before I became a therapist I suffered myself with severe anxiety and depression for the best part of a decade in my twenties, so I know how it feels to be at the mercy of uncontrollable emotions.

If you recognise that you're angry, and **you don't want to be angry** any more, then my message to you is that you're otherwise awesome (because people are when they're happy!), and with a little assistance, you'll remember that about yourself.

Anger Management: Understanding, Healing, Freedom will explain the following: -

* Your brain actually contains two brains. One is rational and logical. The other is instinctive and emotional. Anger is an evolutionary response to feeling threatened. We will explore the role of stress in losing control, how and why the anger response is triggered, and what happens in your brain and body when you lose your temper.

* Suggestions and tools for managing stress including a link to my free downloadable professional anger management hypnosis/relaxation recording.

* Why simply repressing angry responses won't work in the long run as a strategy for being less angry, and can lead to uncontrollable explosions of anger.

* The role of alcohol in anger and the scientific reason that alcohol reduces your ability to retain intellectual control of your anger levels.

* Understanding that attack is a form of defence.

* Recognising that anger is often a cover for emotional vulnerabilities including anxieties, past wounding, and depression. Exploring how these subconscious templates can trigger powerful emotional responses and make it next to impossible to retain intellectual control.

* Using case studies, we will understand the deeper dynamics of these templates, and explain what is necessary to re-write them.

* How and why your brain filters your perception of life negatively, leading you to assume the worst and discount the positives. How to change these perspectives, and start noticing the best in yourself, other people, and the World at large.

* Understanding that anger is generated by the way we interpret events, and the language that we use to explain life to ourselves.

* Exploring why controlling behaviour will get you everything you **don't** want! Understanding how you **can** get what you want without harming yourself or others.

* Why having your "rules" broken will lead to angry responses, and what to do about it.

* Why "venting" your anger does nothing to reduce how angry you feel.

* Dealing with the sense of entitlement and power that anger brings, and recognising why it's ultimately disempowering to you.

* Tackling the addictive and habitual aspects of being chronically angry.

* Explain how being angry is a self-fulfilling prophecy which will only lead to more anger producing situations.

* Understanding how and why "softness controls hardness". Learning to disarm attacks the peaceful way.

* Claiming anger as a positive force for change and determination, and learning to channel anger appropriately.

* The importance of clear heart to heart communication, and how to ask for what you want or need without hostility or defensiveness.

* Understanding what it means to protect yourself using assertiveness, without being aggressive.

* Why "sorry" is such an important word to understand, and the importance of being able to give it as well as receive it.

* Some final words of encouragement!

INTRODUCTION

As a therapist, I have enjoyed working with clients suffering with anger perhaps more than any other conditions I've had to treat. I think that anyone who walks into a therapist's consulting room and asks for help with their anger is hugely courageous. It has always been, for me, a pleasure, and a genuine privilege to be the person who finally explains to the "angry" person that they are not bad! There are reasons that people are angry. The problem is though that the anger is often triggered inappropriately, and then unfortunately misdirected towards the ones we love, undeserving strangers or even ourselves because they are the ones who happen to be there! It's not really about them though. It's about other experiences in life which have left you feeling deeply disempowered and wounded. If you back an animal into a corner, it's going to come out with its teeth bared, and it's going to snarl at you. It won't discriminate either. If you're in the escape route, prepare to be mauled. Attack is considered the strongest form of defence when a mind is in pain.

Angry people are usually not bad people. They are mostly hurt people.

The usual reason that somebody would present for therapy relating to anger is simply to save a relationship. Sadly, anger can be extremely damaging. Terrible things can be done and said in the throes of a red mist. Clients were usually on their last chance by the time they presented for therapy. You may yourself be in a similar situation. If you are, I won't lie. You probably really are on your last chance. I'd tell you that to your face if you walked into my consulting room. This is no time for half-heartedness. It **is** serious, and you won't get control of your anger unless you mean business about sorting this difficulty out, once and for all. You will need to be committed to change, but, it can be done, and it will be my privilege to share with you the understanding you need to get it done. Some of what follows is going to be challenging, but for what it's worth, I want to remind you that you are not your pain, or your anger. You are almost certainly a decent human being with a good heart. You are who you are when you're not angry. Sincerely, I see that, and I want to help you clear those red mists away, and break free from the prison your anger has become.

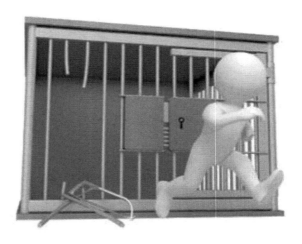

So, please remember...**I am on your side!**

You can learn to control your temper. You can also learn to feel a lot more peaceful in general. I'm going to walk you through what you need to know, and give you the tools you'll need to make a success of it. I sincerely hope that this offering will help you to transform your life, and find peace again.

So, please leave any scepticism or cynicism at the door before coming in, take a moment to commit to learning what you need to know, and we'll get this process underway!

John Crawford – Bristol – June 2016.

CHAPTER ONE – WHAT HAPPENS WHEN YOU LOSE YOUR TEMPER?

Anger and anxiety are nature's mechanisms for making sure we stay alive. Our species has been on the planet for about two million years. We've evolved in the wild, and we've faced continued life-threatening dangers from predatory animals and warring tribes. It's been a matter of survival. Our brains therefore have evolved to respond very powerfully to the presence of perceived threats. Nature has learned that there are three functions necessary to keep us alive. They are "run-away", "stand and fight", and "freeze". You may already be familiar with the shorthand for this. We call it "fight or flight".

You have two brains inside your skull. At the base of the brain is an area called the limbic system. This is what we call the emotional or instinctive brain. It is not a "thinking" brain. It is an "instinctive" brain. It's the animal part of the brain which looks after survival. Wrapped around the limbic system we have the cortex, and at the front of the cortex we have the frontal lobe. The frontal lobe is the part of your brain that is associated with higher intelligence, specifically, the functions of logic, reason, planning, and control. This is what makes you human.

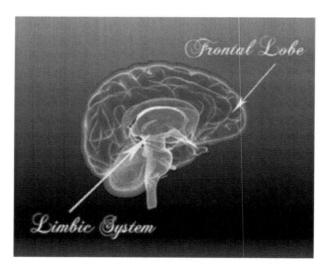

Ordinarily, we navigate life primarily using the frontal lobe to guide us. That means that for the most part, we are using logic and reason to dictate our actions. Biologists recognise that the human "animal" brain is partly hardwired for violence. Though violence is not the only option available to us because we are also hardwired for love and co-operation, it's important to recognise that violence is a natural part of the makeup of all human beings. Usually, this tendency towards violence is safely supressed by the frontal lobe functions of "reason" and "control". In other words, you don't lash out every time someone upsets you. There are circumstances however which can cause our usual control mechanisms to fail. Let's have a look at how this can happen.

When your limbic system brain detects a "threat" in the environment, it sends out an immediate alarm signal which tells the body to ready itself for emergency action. The body instantly releases powerful hormones into the bloodstream, namely cortisol, and adrenaline (epinephrine) which have a strongly stimulant effect on the body. This makes the heart beat faster to supply the limbs with increased oxygen for power. Our skin perspires to cool us and make us more slippery to catch. Our breathing rate becomes shallow and faster so as to bring in more oxygen. Our eyes widen to receive more information. We feel giddy, as blood is pumped away from the brain to the limbs. Our guts feel tense and sick. We become laden with energy which makes us shake and tremble, and **rational thought is put to one side** in favour of instinctual reaction. In short, we become pumped up for fight or flight. Instinct is deemed more powerful in an emergency than thought, so when we are angry or afraid, our brain blocks access to our usual intelligence, meaning literally that we can't think straight. When you lose your temper, this is what's happening. It's often known as "seeing red", which is a pretty accurate description of what is happening. Your usual logic and control, which ordinarily keeps a lid on violent impulses, is temporarily overwhelmed by the stimulant effect of this emotional arousal.

All of this would be hardly noticeable in a life or death situation. We would simply be focussed upon survival. When this response is triggered inappropriately however, we have a problem!

So that, in a nutshell, is what is actually happening when you lose your temper.

THE EFFECTS OF REPRESSING ANGER

So, let's assume that most of the time you are successful in **not** losing your temper. There are lots of irritations throughout the day which get under your skin. Before you leave the house in the morning, you can't find your car keys. You've got ten minutes, and you've searched everywhere. "God dammit! Where the f*** are my keys?!" With keys finally found down the side of the sofa, you rush out the door, now aware that you might be late for work. The pressure is on. You're keen now to avoid the traffic, but it's already building up. You've lost your early advantage. On your way to work, another driver jumps the queue and makes you miss the green traffic light. You seethe for a while. You hurry to your desk ten minutes late, apologising to your manager, feeling slightly ashamed, and temporarily disliked. Later, a customer is rude to you. You grit your teeth, and smile sweetly. As you drive home at the end of your busy day, you suddenly remember that you haven't renewed your home insurance. A jolt of alarm goes through your body as you realise that if your house burnt down today you'd be screwed! You make a mental note that you must get that done immediately. But, money is tight right now, and a surge of frustration enters your mind as you feel the overload of the hundred and one things that need attention, and financing! And so, on it goes....

This is life, right? There's nothing extraordinary about this. You have better days some days, but in one way or another, life often contains these daily irritations. When you're at your best you manage to take it all in your stride. But, it doesn't last. One day you get out of the wrong side of the bed and it's just a bad day from the first moment. Your patience has worn thin, and it seems like it is just one thing after another. With every irritation you can feel that pressure building up, and it's that day, when you get home, that all hell is let loose.

What has happened? Well, you know that saying "I've had it up to here!"? It turns out that's an accurate description of this process. Your nervous system is like a container, a bucket, and it has a limited capacity. When we're calm and relaxed, this bucket has spare capacity. Sometimes however, the volume of "stress" going into our bucket can cause it overload. The volume of stress that our bucket contains at any given moment will dictate how much "control" we have. As the bucket overfills we become more and more overwhelmed by that limbic system arousal, which means that our usual functions of reason and control become less and less able to suppress the violent impulses. Like a pressure cooker without a safety valve, at some point, it just blows! We lose control, and there is your hell breaking loose.

The rule is that where there is emotional arousal, there must also be discharge of that energy. So, with every irritation which you can't express outwardly, there must be repression of that energy. This is a natural process. We have always had to repress anger. Even our earliest ancestors had to get along with each other. Survival would not have been possible without co-operation. Thankfully then, we have a mechanism which allows safe discharge of that repressed energy. That is sleep.

When you sleep, your brain organises your experiences by deciding what can be deleted, what needs to stay immediately, and what needs to be retained long term. We experience this process as dreaming. If you pay attention to your dreams, you will notice that your dreams are often a metaphorical replaying of certain situations or concerns relating to your recent experiences. This is your brains way of sifting through the themes which are currently playing out for you in life. We spend approximately twenty five percent of our time asleep dreaming (Rapid Eye Movement sleep), and the other seventy five percent in slow-wave sleep, which is restful and recuperative. This process empties your stress bucket. Or, at least it should. Problems arise when there's too much daily stress going into the bucket. Then the system can become overloaded, and our sleep cycle can't take care of it all in one go. Then we experience longer period of REM sleep which is not restful. Studies show that the brain is more active when we are in REM sleep than when we are awake, so REM sleep is necessary, but not restful. You would experience this as intense dreams or nightmares, and restless sleep. Then we wake up with our bucket still full of some of yesterday's stresses. In addition to an unemptied bucket, we're also more tired because we've had less restful sleep, and this makes us more prone to being more easily irritated. You can see then how this can become a negative cycle which leads to continued emotional overload.

Remember that the more overloaded your bucket becomes, the less "control" your logical brain is able to exert upon the emotional brain, and what that means in practice is that your performance suffers in just about every conceivable way. This is not conducive to improving matters. It simply makes things worse.

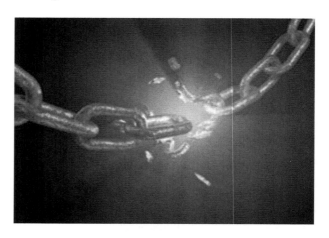

You become more tired, more irritable, and less productive. In short, you're simply not coping as well as you usually would. This can then lead to the creation of further stressful circumstances which deepen your distress. Now that bad day becomes a really bad day. You're searching for your keys so frantically that you break the kitchen drawer as you yank it open. You're so incensed by the driver that pushed in front of you that you sound your horn for ten seconds solid while everyone stares at you, making you feel hated by the World. Instead of apologising to the boss for being ten minutes late, you mutter under your breath, and they hear it. There goes your promotion. You are sarcastic and obstructive with your rude customer, who then files a complaint about you, and by the time you get home you're just about ready to blow. Your partner asks gently "Have you sorted out the house insurance yet?", and Blam! Who gets it? Things are said and done which end up with you hating yourself, and probably with your partner hating you for a bit too.

To my mind, this is a really sad story. The uninformed onlooker might have no sympathy. You're the one that blew up at your partner for no reason at all. What's the matter with you? Get a grip! But clearly, that's not the full story. So, you may ask, "Why me? It seems like most people can control their temper, and they have stresses too, so there must be something wrong with ME!?"

ALCOHOL

It's not only stress which can cause us to blow. Alcohol Concern, a leading alcohol harm-prevention charity tells us: -

* *Victims (of violence) believed the offender(s) to be under the influence of alcohol in over half (53%) of all violent incidents, or 704,000 offences.*

More than half of all violence happens not only as a result of alcohol, but probably **because** of alcohol. Here's another statistic which backs this up: -

* *Twenty nine percent of all violent incidents in 2013–14 took place in or around a pub or club. This rises to 42% for stranger violence. Over two thirds (68%) of violent offences occur in the evening or at night.*

What is it about alcohol then which causes so much anger and violence? Well, let's go back to the brain for a moment. Under normal (sober) conditions the limbic system is kept in check by the reasoning brain, the frontal lobes. We literally exercise constant control over our emotions on a minute by minute, day by day basis. Providing we are not suffering with chronic anger or huge overloads of stress, the frontal lobes do a pretty good job of keeping us sailing through the irritating stuff, and letting it wash over us. We do this without too much effort. While we may feel the odd irritation rising, our logical brain very quickly rationalises the situation and keeps everything in its proper perspective. It's an equilibrium which is maintained naturally and automatically. When this system is functioning well, we're much less likely to lose our cool.

The frontal lobes are all about **control**. We know this to be the case because people who have frontal lobe brain damage have great difficulty in these areas. Common characteristics of damage to the frontal lobes also include risk taking, rule breaking, and difficulty in interpreting feedback from the environment. In other words, being somewhat oblivious to what's going on around you, and having a lack of awareness of the future consequences of immediate actions. Does this sound familiar? It should. This is what happens to a human being when they become very drunk on alcohol too. There's a joke which says "I'd rather have a bottle in front of me than have a frontal lobotomy". It's ironic then that alcohol pretty much **is** a frontal lobotomy, temporarily at least.

The very first thing to be affected by alcohol consumption is the frontal lobe area of the brain. In short, alcohol attacks the brain's ability to use logic, reason, planning, and control. In small doses this is usually fun. It's nice to say "screw it" for a few hours. For many people, that's exactly what alcohol is; a few hours of forgetting about responsibilities, breaking some social rules by being a little more animated than is usually allowed, and eating some junk food at the end of the night. These are our happy drunks. Not everyone is a happy drunk though. Some people have a Jekyll and Hyde experience. For them, alcohol reveals a darker self, often with a personality all of its own. Some alcohol experts suggest that people who experience a sudden shift from one self to another when under the influence of alcohol are "alcoholic" by definition, and are therefore better off avoiding alcohol use altogether. This is probably good advice, but the important thing to understand about the relationship between alcohol and anger is that alcohol reduces intellectual control, and increases limbic system dominance. What that means in practical terms is that the frontal lobes will fail to restrain the limbic system impulses. This will be fine if you don't have easily triggered anger responses, or a seething seam of unexpressed anger lurking just beneath the surface, but for those who do, alcohol use is like opening the gate of the lion's enclosure. Chaos is likely to ensue.

We're going to continue now to explore what anger is all about, and later, how you can permanently reduce the sensitivity of those triggers, and cool the boiling pot. The chances are that when you successfully resolve your reasons for anger generally, you will also experience a significant change in what happens for you when you use alcohol. Your alter-ego should take on a much gentler form. With that said however, for some people, anger is not really the problem; alcohol is. Some people just don't function well on alcohol, and probably never will. If you successfully work through your anger difficulties, only to find that you become a monster when you drink, then there's only one thing for it. The booze will have to go. I know that is much easier said than done, and it's not something this book will tackle, but there are many organisations which will help you with alcohol-related problems. If you recognise that alcohol is central to your problem, don't be afraid to pick up the phone and speak to someone. It can be done.

CHAPTER TWO - WHY AM I SO ANGRY?

There are a number of answers to this question:-

* As just briefly discussed, it may simply be that your stress levels generally are overloaded. When stress levels are overloaded, we can easily become anxious or depressed too, and anger can be a part of those responses. We'll be looking at practical strategies for reducing stress levels later.

* You could be angry because you have been hurt by life, and here we're not just talking about the irritations we've just discussed. We're talking about true wounding. This can make a person very "defensive", and as we'll explore in a moment, attack is seen by a wounded mind as the best form of defence.

* Another very common reason for anger is that you may have a way of explaining life's events to yourself which causes **unnecessary** emotional arousal. This is known as interpretational style, or how you "frame" things. This can include anger as a habit, and an addiction. I'll explain more in a bit.

* Your "rules" are being broken.

* Somebody is taking something from you which you don't wish to give, or someone/something (i.e an institution) is "laying something on you" that you don't wish to receive.

* You feel like you don't have enough "control".

* You are being attacked, or treated unjustly.

We've just looked at stress levels, so let's consider how being hurt can cause anger too.

ATTACK IS THE BEST FORM OF DEFENCE

In order to fully understand this, it's first necessary to understand the role of the conscious mind versus the subconscious mind. Your conscious mind contains everything that you know you know. Your subconscious mind contains things you know, but don't know that you know. If that sounds confusing, stay with me, I'll explain using an example.

James (a fictional character), is a really nice guy. He has a great job, a loving wife, and is a wonderful dad. There's just one problem. He can't stand people lying to him, and he can't stand being called a liar. In fact, if anyone ever even insinuates that he might be inaccurate in his reporting of a situation he just loses it. A deep rage takes over. It's like he's possessed. He can't understand it. It's the sole cause of unhappiness in his life. He once found himself stood over his wife with his hand raised, after she insisted that he had taken money from the joint bank account which he knew he hadn't. This is a memory for which he remains deeply ashamed. It haunts him daily.

James places great value on his integrity. It's just always been really important to him. Even despite his shame, he still becomes deeply enraged if he senses any distrust from his wife. Consciously, James believes that a person's integrity is their worth. He believes that people who don't value integrity, simply don't value themselves. He goes to extraordinary lengths to make sure that his integrity is unquestionable. It's just the way it is in James' world. So that's what James knows

21

consciously. He believes that he has arrived at that conclusion through careful thought about what is right and what's wrong. He has, he believes, chosen to be a person of integrity, and he's happy with that decision....except for the anger.....he could do without the anger.

What James doesn't remember though is an event. Actually, it's more accurate to say that James does remember the event, but he doesn't actually recognise how deeply he was affected by the event. One day, when James was six years old, he woke up on a Saturday morning, and his parents were having a blazing row. He was deeply shocked. He'd seen his parents bickering before, but now he could hear screams coming from the kitchen. He was really frightened. It sounded like they might kill each other. He crept to the top of the stairs. He heard his Dad say some terrible words, and he heard his Mum crying. Then he heard his Dad say "F*** you. If you can't tell the f*****g truth, then we're finished". Then he heard the door slam, and he just sat there shocked as his Mum sobbed downstairs. His mind went into overdrive. Was Dad coming back? Was life as he knew it about to end? It felt like the end of the World to him. Later that evening his Dad was back and although there was a funny feeling in the house, he saw them cuddling again, and he felt safe again...sort of. Twenty three years later and they're still together now.

Consciously then, James remembers this simply as an awful row that scared him. What he has failed to remember are the **words** that were spoken. "If you can't tell the truth, then we're finished". Because James was in shock at the time, his mind became highly "suggestible". It's a fact that states of shock are highly hypnosis-like. He was consciously focussed on the possibility that his dad was gone forever, but what registered **subconsciously** was the formula. That formula was as follows: **"When people don't tell the truth, very bad things happen!"**

Life returned to normal soon after and a week later James had just about forgotten about the terrible row. He never saw his parents have another row like that again. Subconsciously though, that formula remained a powerfully guiding principle in James' life. Now, when James experiences a situation in which someone is lying to him, or in which he himself is accused of lying, he re-experiences all of that fear that he felt as he listened to his parents about to kill each other on that fateful day. His subconscious mind sends him a message. "THIS MUST NOT BE ALLOWED TO HAPPEN!!" He experiences this as a flood of powerful feelings of being very threatened. The response then, is anger. He can't run away. There's only one option left. He must stand and fight. This situation **must** be extinguished immediately. Defence has become attack. Hopefully, you can now see how this principle operates?

When viewed from this perspective, we can begin to understand that anger is actually a cover for anxiety in some cases. Behind some anger is fear.

There are other angles on this theme too. In the above example it's purely fear which has been established as the cause of anger. It's entirely possible though for the same principle to be applied to anger itself. Let's take a real world case study for this one. I'm going to change the names and details for the sake of confidentiality, but it was an interesting case which I enjoyed solving, and I'd like to share it with you.

Mark came to me with an eating problem, specifically, a chocolate problem. He simply couldn't stop eating it. But, when he did eat it, he wasn't enjoying it. He would simply scoff it, a big bar at a time, and he said he was aware of a feeling of anger within him as he did so. He hated himself for the behaviour, but there was an aspect of "screw it!" every time he did it. I'll cut a long story short. I worked with him using hypnotherapy. We tuned in on that angry feeling and I asked him within the hypnotic state to follow that feeling back to the first time he'd ever felt it. Bingo! He relayed a story. Easter was approaching, and his Mum had promised him that he could have an Easter egg, come the big day, and he'd spent days before in a state of excitement, pondering on which egg he would choose. The day arrived and they drove to the shops with great excitement. He got into the store and marvelled at the fantastic assortment of colours and themes. He was thrilled. As he was choosing his egg though, his mum was having other ideas. She was looking at the weight of the chocolate in the eggs, and then looking at the bars on the counter and concluded that the eggs were bad value for money! She couldn't be swayed on this, and Mark consequently left the shop with a great big bar of dairy milk. He said he remembered sitting in the back of the car on the drive home with this huge sense of disappointment and anger. He took the (stupid) bar of chocolate, unwrapped it, and started angrily scoffing it, resenting every bite!

We resolved the chocolate eating problem. Once Mark understood the source of his anger, and the reason for his binges, he was able to tackle the problem. The subconscious mind was re-running the programme in an attempt to make it somehow "right". But, of course, it was never right, because it wasn't really about chocolate. It was about disappointment and betrayal. That sounds like strong words to say about an Easter egg, but to a seven year old, that's important stuff! We worked together to speak to his inner seven year old, and explain that his mum really did love him, and that it was a terrible mistake on her part. She didn't know how upset that had made him, and Mark communicated to his younger self that he would always make sure that he was listened to from this point forwards. Mark's homework then was to spend regular daily time in meditation "being" with his seven year old self, eating Easter eggs together! In this case, if attack is defence, it was chocolate that was being attacked! Anger can be easily misplaced. So, that's an interesting story, but it's an unusual one too. Let's have a look at something a bit more common with another fictional example:-

Pete left home at the age of seventeen. He was glad to get away. It wasn't anything he could put his finger on exactly. To everyone else his parents seemed like lovely people, but they just had this way of making him feel undermined. Little comments, often disguised as jokes, were the ones that really got to him. He'd tried really hard to please them, but they always seemed distracted. His mum used to say "Your Dad and I were going to live in Australia....but we never got there because you came along", and then she'd laugh. Pete remembers bringing home his school report. It was full of A's and his mum said "Oooh....look at you....Clever Clogs!" She was joking, but Pete didn't think it was funny. For as long as he could remember he'd felt tolerated, but not really wanted. He knew this because he often caught "that" look from his Mum. When he was older he knew what it meant. It was displeasure. He hated that look. It made him feel really ugly.

When Pete was nineteen, he met the love of his life. Karen was perfect in every way to Pete's eyes. It was great. He'd never been happier. They moved in together, and Pete got a new job in sales, but after a while he started to notice a really bad feeling. Sometimes, Karen would ask Pete not to leave wet bath towels on the floor, and Pete would feel violently attacked. He'd feel his anger rising: "Fine! But, while we're at it, can you make sure you clean up your dishes before you leave for work?!" At first, it was just the odd thing, but over time, the feelings got worse, and so did the fights. A year later Karen moved out.

So, what happened here? It's sort of complicated. Let me clarify. Every child craves positive reinforcement from their parents/carers. It's not just a want, it's a need. When a child doesn't receive the message "You are good enough, you are wanted, and loved", that child's heart will metaphorically be broken. They will presume that it's THEIR fault. Child logic will say, "If my parents do not want me, then there must be something wrong with me. I must be a bad person. I must be unlovable". They may never have this thought in words, but they will feel it. If they then go on to try harder to please their parents without positive result they will eventually feel "crushed". This experience is so awful and painful that the subconscious mind will create two templates of experience (belief) from such an upbringing. The first reads "You must never let anyone make you feel like your parents made you feel ever again." The second reads something along the lines of "All efforts to be loved will eventually end in you realising that you are unlovable."

When Pete met Karen, he was floating on a cloud of bliss. When love first blossoms we have a honeymoon period. This means that we are drunk on love, and willing to overlook the faults and idiosyncrasies of our partner, but this doesn't last forever. At some point the hypnotic effect of adoration wanes, and in order for the relationship to mature the next phase involves a sobering-up period where our differences come into view. In the first six months of their relationship Pete felt **unconditionally** loved for the first time in his life. As the effects of infatuation diminished, Karen took a step towards attempting to address their incompatibilities. It was here that Pete had his buttons pushed. Pete's upbringing left him with a strong feeling that he was ultimately unlovable. Karen's requests were perfectly reasonable. She wanted to live in a house which had some order to it. That's not what Pete heard though. When Karen asked him to pick up his wet towels, what Pete heard was "You're not good enough". When Karen talked to Pete about their financial situation being a bit stretched, what Pete heard was "You're not good enough". When Karen told Pete he was being rather defensive every time they spoke, what Pete heard was "You're not good enough!"

So, why is anger about hurt here? Pete's subconscious mind is "hyper-vigilant" to the presence of perceived criticism. As in earlier examples, attack is the best form of defence. Instead of hearing the perfectly reasonable points that Karen is airing for discussion or action, his emotional mind has agendas. The first is "You must never let anyone make you feel like your parents made you feel ever again." So, instead of thinking "That's a fair point. I can see why that would annoy Karen", Pete finds himself overwhelmed by an angry limbic system response which causes him to retaliate with an attack. Karen wasn't attacking him. She was just asking him to maintain some order in the home, but his limbic system doesn't understand this. All it knows is that nobody should ever make him feel as **hurt** as his parents did. Karen's requests feel very similar to the constant undermining he experienced early in life and anger follows.

If this wasn't bad enough, we also have the second subconscious agenda: "All efforts to be loved will eventually end in you realising that you are unlovable." Once the arguments begin, Pete's subconscious mind sees only one possible outcome. That's something along the lines of "No matter what I do, this person is never really going to love me. All they do is criticize me. I may as well end it now and save myself the pain." Subconsciously, in a passive-aggressive demonstration of his independence Pete makes even less effort to keep the house tidy. He finds himself regarding Karen with a certain level of contempt. He says she is always nagging him. He stops listening. In short, his subconscious mind sabotages the relationship. The outcome is that eventually Karen can't make it work. She is forced to leave. At this point Pete is firmly convinced that it was Karen's nagging that caused their relationship to fail. Six months later he meets Natalie. She's perfect....at first! He still doesn't pick up his towels. Then, she starts nagging......

To the subconscious mind ANYTHING is better than feeling the pain of the past.

We need to have some empathy for poor Pete. While it is very definitely his responsibility to deal with these angry triggers, we also can recognise that he is somewhat at the mercy of his subconscious programming. This is far more powerful than his will. Telling it straight, he can have all the good will in the world, but if he fails to recognise the problem and work through it, he is doomed to repeat the pattern. It's not just towels either. He can't fix it by deciding to pick up his towels. If it's not that, it will be something else. It's not Pete's fault that he is the way he is. He has our empathy. But, unfortunately, it is now his responsibility to fix the problem. If Pete's story resonates with you, stay with me, we'll be moving on to resolutions shortly!

DIRTY FILTERS CAUSE DIRTY PERCEPTION

Picture this. I'm walking along the street. I see a guy coming towards me on the other side of the road, and I notice his jacket. It's really unusual, and I'm taken with the smart colour patches. I'm thinking to myself "Wow, that's a nice jacket!" I catch his eye, and give a little smile before looking away. As we pass I notice he's still looking at me, but he's scowling suspiciously.

If we step into his mind for a moment, what's going on here? He's seeing this guy looking over. It makes him uncomfortable. He becomes angry. His subconscious programme kicks into action. His first thought is, "What are you f*****g looking at?!" This might sound extreme, but actually there are many people walking around who will react negatively to being looked at. In some cases, sadly, it can be the beginning of a nasty confrontation, especially when people are drunk.

So let's look at the situation objectively. My intention is admiration of his jacket. His subconscious mind however, immediately sees threat. Why? Well, if we think about the examples given earlier we can deduce that this person's experience has produced a subconscious programme that says "The World is a hostile place." He's expecting my attention to be hostile, so he responds with anger.

Cognitive Behavioural Therapy recognises that all perception is subjective. In other words: -

I do not see things as they are. I see them as I am.

We all have filters through which we view ourselves, the world, and other people. These are called Schemata. Essentially, these schemata filter all incoming information according to our preconceived beliefs and expectations. Schemata tend to be "fixed", meaning that once we hold a certain view, it is not easily changed. These filters have the effect of making the World fit in with our expectations, as opposed to us changing our expectations to match the World.

In practice, this means that incoming information which does not fit with our pre-conceived idea of how things are, is disregarded. It also means that we will actively seek out experience which does match with our own beliefs. If you're a Conservative voter, you'll probably read the Daily Mail. If you're a liberal, you'll prefer The Guardian. As far as the subconscious mind is concerned, certainty is a great asset. None of us would want to wake up one morning and suddenly have everything we know thrown into question. That would be confusing, and disconcerting. So, the subconscious mind favours certainty, and seeks out experience which reinforces that certainty, even if that certainty is inaccurate or unhelpful. That's why we have the saying "You can't teach an old dog new tricks." We're going to be looking in detail at why this particular cause of anger is so damaging in Chapter Three.

We've looked in detail then at the way in which our past experiences and environments may have shaped our automatic responses, and we've noted that these can be powerful **involuntary** reactions which are driven by subconscious fears and hurts. There are other ways in which anger can dominate our lives.

INTERPRETATIONAL STYLE

Nothing is anything until we decide it is so. The way we interpret events will dictate how we feel about them. Our interpretational style is rooted in our upbringing and experience too, but our interpretational style can also be of our own doing. When it is, we are less the victims of circumstance, and more the architects of our own fate. Sometimes, we ourselves have arrived at cynical or distrustful ways of viewing the world, ourselves, or others because we have chosen to do so. There may still be good reasons that we have arrived at such conclusions, but as the Dalai Lama pointed out, hate and anger themselves are the true enemy because they will destroy **your** peace.

"Anger is like a hot rock that you intend to throw at someone else. In the end, the person it burns is you."

You may or may not know that the Dalai Lama lives in India following exile from his homeland in Tibet in 1959. He said that after a period of being angry about the invasion of the Chinese Communist regime into Tibet, he realised that his sense of anger and injustice was doing him more harm than the invasion itself, and he undertook practice to find his peace with the situation. This is a good example of a person "choosing" to change their perspective on an anger provoking injustice, and the reasoning is sound. It doesn't feel fair intuitively. It isn't fair! Sometimes our anger is entirely justified, but where there are situations beyond our control, we are faced with two options. We can become angry, bitter, stressed, and cynical, or we can choose to actively work on softening. We need to understand that holding on too tightly to our sometimes righteous indignation means that our aggressor can hurt us twice! Here's a quick story from my own life a few weeks back: -

As I drove to my destination this morning, a driver coming in the opposite direction decided to overtake the car in front at high speed, and it appeared to me that as he swerved out and back in again, only to have to slam on his brakes because there was another car in front of him again, that he accelerated so hard that he very nearly lost control of his car. Had he done so I almost certainly would have been hit head on, as his angle meant he was driving straight towards me! I felt a surge of anger, no... outrage....and various cursing expletives left my mouth. A stranger just risked my life...for what?! To get one car ahead?! Morally, my outrage was completely justified. His risk taking was stupid, reckless, thoughtless, and selfish, and a moment of madness could have ruined many lives. He was obviously unable to control his emotions and almost his car too as a result. He was clearly irritated by the slowness of the driver in front, and his impatience got the better of him. But, when I was still seething five minutes later, I asked myself a question. If I was still angry, wasn't I, in some way guilty of the same offence? Was my hatred and disgust getting the better of me? Was I not guilty of failing to control MY emotions? I remembered Ram Dass had said "I like to keep a picture of my enemy on my altar to remind me how far I still have to go." If this sounds cryptic, he was referring to this principle of learning to see the World with peaceful filters, that is, without hate, and recognising that this is deeply challenging. So, I took some deep breaths, and I gave myself permission to let it go. I didn't magically return to my pre-incident jolliness. It still took a while, but twenty minutes later I was having a cup of tea with my friend and chatting about cats! It was the act of initiating the decision to remember that I'm not perfect either which made the difference. Choosing to let it go wasn't easy. Neither was challenging my own sense of **righteousness**. It was actually quite painful. The truth is I've made poor decisions too. I will do so again. Every fibre of my being wanted to stay mad by making him wrong and me right. I was able to consider for the moment though that yes, it was a reckless and selfish behaviour by him which I took personally, but maybe it was unusual for him too. The nameless, faceless car is a perfect screen upon which to project all the anger of all the times that people have behaved badly towards you, so the feeling can be very much one of imagining the driver as the **worst** person in the World!

It's almost certainly not the case. Maybe he was really late for a life-changing meeting and was under great stress? Maybe he was trying to get to the hospital to see his dying daughter? Maybe his house was being repossessed and his life was falling apart? Maybe he really was just an idiot. There could have been all sorts of reasons that he'd lost his sense of control. The fact is though, I'll never know.

None of this condones the behaviour, but I could at least soften my position by recognising that on another day, under different circumstances, that car could have been mine. Who hasn't cursed at someone who didn't indicate at a roundabout? But, haven't you done it too in a moment of absent-mindedness, hurry, or stress? We need to recognise that anger doesn't serve much of a purpose most of the time other than to make us…well…angry!

Regardless of the circumstances, ultimately it boiled down to the logical conclusion that it was me who was experiencing the stress, not him. He was probably blissfully unaware that he'd even upset anyone. My choice was to carry it around all day, or I could let it go.

Letting it go doesn't mean <u>condoning</u> an action. It just means refusing to beat yourself with the stick you picked up to defend yourself!

So, the event is the event, but how you choose to interpret that event is up to you! Seeing the worst in things is likely to cause you to feel angrier.

THE CONTROL IT OR LOSE IT MISTAKE

One of the uglier faces of anger is that of "controlling" behaviour. This problem can actually be a form of OCD (Obsessive Compulsive Disorder). There are a number of areas that people can obsess about. These include, but are not limited to worry about death, illness, reputation, and jealousy. Jealousy is experienced as a strong persistent feeling that something you love will be taken from you. Though there **could** be dishonesty taking place that you should be concerned about, jealousy is usually a form of paranoia. The limbic system brain has become hyper-vigilant because of high stress levels and is now overestimating the perceived risk of loss. In this hyper-vigilant state, the limbic system attaches unnecessary meaning to every small detail, and the jealousy sufferer will find it very difficult to convince him or herself that the loss is not imminent. This feeling of imminent loss will almost certainly root back to earlier wounding as we just discussed. So, growing up in a situation where you felt constantly starved of any "control", and suffered as a result, will make you do just about anything to make sure you never experience having no control ever again. Strongly emotive experiences of being abandoned at a young age may have the same effect. The main problem is that these feelings can drive people to become "controlling". Sadly, many cases of domestic abuse are driven by this need to control a partner. The further you venture into controlling a partner, the angrier you will become. You are effectively sending a message to your limbic system which says that you "agree" with its assessment that you are about to lose the love of your life, and because there is a feedback loop between what you "feel" and what you "believe", your limbic system takes your endorsement as good reason to continue providing you with that terrible jealous emotion. This simply deepens your sense that something is wrong. You are then compelled to check up on your partner obsessively, and "control" their movements and thoughts. It can't work. No relationship can thrive in such a stifling environment. Eventually your behaviour is so difficult to live with that your partner leaves, and you get the very thing you were trying to avoid happening. We'll be taking a look at a case study of this self-fulfilling prophecy in Chapter Three with Daniella.

SOMEONE BROKE YOUR RULES

It was late in life that somebody explained this to me. I'd never really thought about it before it was pointed out. We get angry when someone, or something, breaks our "rules". If we look back at my earlier example, the reckless driver broke my rule of, "You **should not** drive dangerously and risk other peoples' lives". It's a fair enough one. Morally it's completely justified. Tragically, live **are** ruined by reckless drivers. Anger is an appropriate response. Holding on to it, is not.

"Rules" then, are there to create order in a chaotic world. The thirty miles per hour speed limit is there to save lives. Texting while driving is more dangerous than drink driving. That's why most of us feel angry when we see someone doing it. We generally hold rules in high regard. But, some rules are inaccurate and outdated. Consider the many cultural rules which have been updated over the years. Homosexuality was a criminal offence with sodomy carrying a possible life sentence in jail in the UK until 1967. In 2016, same sex marriage is legally recognised by the UK State. Homosexuality is still illegal in no less than seventy six countries, most of which are in the "developing world". In the United States, racial segregation was the norm for decades, but was abolished (in law) in 1964. Most people agree it was a terrible and oppressive affair. Of course, these problems are far from over today. Approximately one in six federal inmates in the US prison system are serving time for Marijuana related offences, but Marijuana is now legal in a number of US States for recreational use. Work that one out?! Times change, and so do our values. Not everyone will agree with the changes, and therein is the root of the problem. Many rules we agree upon, but some we do not. Most decent people will agree that "Thou shalt not kill" is a pretty fundamental rule for order to prevail. Most of us don't steal either. So that's all nice and tidy. Stealing is wrong, killing is wrong. You get angry when you witness it. Good. That's entirely appropriate.

Problems begin in the grey areas between black and white. Let me recount a quick story to illustrate this point. Back in 1991, I travelled to California to make a new life with my girlfriend (now my wife). We had next to nothing. Just a small amount of savings and our plan was not well considered. Still, a friend of hers had agreed to put us up for a short time while we got ourselves sorted out. It was very chaotic, but we loved each other and would do anything to be together. After about a week or so, one day we arrived back at the apartment, and all of our belongings were thrown onto the front porch. We'd been evicted! We were soon in discussion with our friend, and one of the reasons she'd become so angry was because a frying pan had not been washed up. She felt we were disrespecting her generosity. There was no changing her mind. We found ourselves homeless. The rest of the story is another book that will probably never be written. The crazy thing is though I'd had every intention of being super respectful of her generosity. Indeed, I couldn't thank her enough for the help.

Here's what had happened. Growing up in 1970's London where money was tight, and thrift was rife, my parents kept a frying pan on the stove with oil in it. Much like a chip pan, this oil was not changed after every use. It was kept for a few cooks and then washed and changed. To me, that was just what you did with a frying pan. You left it on the stove with oil in it. So, what it boiled down to was simply that we had different "rules" about what to do with a frying pan after you've used it. It made her angry enough to literally throw us out onto the street.

So, not all rule books match! Let's take something a little more usual as an example. Suppose I'm one of those laid back types. When I say I'll meet you for coffee **about** midday, what I actually mean is sometime **around** midday. That's because I don't like to pin myself down too tightly. I might have to wait for you. You might have to wait for me. Or, we might both arrive at the same time. It's all good. I mean you're pretty laid back too, right? In my mind, if you're there first, you can sit down, order a coffee, read the paper, and all will be well. I'll buy more coffees when I get there and we'll catch up. It doesn't occur to me that this might actually annoy you. I just assume that everyone is relaxed about timings as I am. I see the fact that we can be loose about arrangements as an indication of our good friendship. We make allowances for each other. It wouldn't bother me if you were late. I know people get delayed sometimes. I do try to get there for midday but I am a little disorganised. I don't stress because I'm sure you wouldn't want me to. At 12.10 I'm still not there, and you are becoming increasingly exasperated. By the time I arrive at 12.15, waving and saying Hi as though nothing has happened, you're so worked up you can't even hide it!

What has actually happened here? Why are you so worked up? Well, you've had a number of rules broken. Here they are: -

* You **should always** leave extra time to allow for delays.

* Friends who care about each other **should** show their consideration by having the **common courtesy** to arrive as arranged.

* You **shouldn't** assume that I have all the time in the World!

Note the bold words. **Should and shouldn't** are the primary cause of distress because on each point I have broken your rule. I didn't leave extra time for delays. I didn't show you consideration and common courtesy by arriving at the arranged time, and I did assume that you had as much time as I do. What you are failing to recognise however is that in my rulebook being fifteen minutes late to an informal friendly arrangement doesn't constitute a lack of respect for you. I have a blind spot here. Our rules are simply different. In essence then, when something "should" be a certain way, and then it's not, it will create emotional disturbance. More often than not, this will be anger and/or frustration.

Now, pause for a moment and think about the last time you got angry. Which of your rules were broken?

35

Later, we're going to look at solutions. I want to present the solutions in the second half of the book so that you can see how they all work together, and so that they will be fresh in your mind. We'll come back to your answer then.

WHAT'S MINE AIN'T YOURS, AND WHAT'S YOURS YOU CAN KEEP!

How would you feel about a paycut? How do you feel when someone asks you for too many favours? What do you think when someone borrows something from you and doesn't return it? Worse still, how do you feel when someone steals your bike, your jewellery, or your wallet? It's not deep joy, and loving kindness is it? Anger is a natural response to having something taken from you when you didn't intend to give it.

Then we have the inverse of being taken from, which is having something given to you that you don't wish to receive. This could take many forms including unwanted responsibility, slander against your good name, indoctrination, someone else's bitterness, a bad debt, undeserved guilt, being accused of something you didn't do, being made to feel ashamed for something you felt okay about, or even just having to listen endlessly to your friend's negativity. It's all a form of being "dumped upon" and mostly it's to do with other people's opinions and "stuff".

ANGER AS A POSITIVE FORCE

Not all anger is destructive. Anger can be a positive transformational force. Indeed, the World would probably still be in the dark ages without it! Anger challenges injustice, and gives us the drive to act courageously in the face of difficult and uncomfortable circumstances.

On December 1st 1955, Rosa Parks, an African American, refused to vacate her seat at the back of the bus when the white section of the segregated bus she was travelling on became full. Though she was not the first person to do this, her stand against oppression, and subsequent arrest for civil disobedience became a powerful rallying symbol for black Americans tired of being treated as second class citizens. Rosa knew she would be arrested. She did it anyway. Only anger has the power to summon such courage.

Anger can help us to transform those aspects of our lives which are not working. Anger can provide the mammoth power needed to:-

* Leave an unhappy relationship.

* Find another job.

* Take action against the school/workplace bully.

* Fight social injustice.

* Refuse to allow people to treat you badly.

* Ask for deserved recognition (i.e a payrise).

* Lose weight.

* Stop misusing drugs or alcohol.

Anger therefore, is necessary, and valuable to us as human beings. Without it we would be quivering doormats with no control over our destinies. Long live anger! Let's just make sure it's channelled, and expressed **appropriately.**

CHAPTER THREE – BEING ANGRY MAKES YOU MORE ANGRY

Consider that anger is an evolutionary response to threat. There is therefore a reasonable expectation that you may sustain damage. The body recognises that if you were to sustain damage, you would still need to continue fighting until your opponent was disabled enough for you to make an escape. So, in addition to those stimulant hormones which pump you up to become unusually powerful, the body also releases natural pain killing chemicals into the bloodstream in **anticipation** of wounding. These natural pain killers are in the same chemical family as heroin. They are opioids. These chemicals can make you feel invincible. When these powerful chemicals course through your veins, your pain threshold will increase dramatically. In emergency situations we can become literally numb. Most people have experienced this at some point. When you have an accident that causes damage, the first thing you feel is shock and numbness. It's only after you have walked to safety on your broken leg that you become aware of the full agony of the break. I've never experienced it, but apparently heroin makes human beings feel pretty amazing for a short time. We all know how addictive heroin is. It's not difficult to see then, how we can become addicted to anger, when being angry releases a free shot of opioids into your bloodstream!

Anger therefore offers an opportunity to feel both **powerful**, and **pleasurable**. Like any drug, that "high" can feel so good that it becomes difficult to resist repeating the experience. The interesting thing is that the more "disempowered" you feel generally, the more likely you are to want or need that experience of being "powerful" more often. If your life generally doesn't have much pleasure in it, then the lure of those opioids also increases. This is important to understand. I have worked with ex-drug addicts who have recounted terrible stories of how they have betrayed their friends, stolen from their parents, and wreaked havoc on the community to get their hands on drugs. These were not bad people. They often came to me for help with resolving their remorse and anxiety about what they had done. Their need for drugs made them do bad things...just like anger does. If you're angry every day, in some ways, you're an addict. Ponder on this for a moment. What will it take to break the addiction? It's not going to happen without your intervention. It's going to be at least as difficult as quitting any drug or habit. A failure to get to grips with the challenge is going to mean that you fail to change it. We're going to need some determination! That means you need to "own" the problem, and take responsibility for its resolution.

A Sense Of Entitlement

Anger is not an easy emotion to handle. One obstacle to becoming less angry is our sense of entitlement to the feeling. When you are angry, it feels justified, but as we've explored, there are many ways in which anger can be triggered inappropriately and unnecessarily. We spoke earlier about interpretational style. This sense of entitlement comes under that heading. Today, in 2016, we are seeing unprecedented levels of corporate and state corruption. As I write, the NHS is being sold off to dubious healthcare providers. The largest companies in the World are paying little to no corporation tax to the UK, and we have had eight years of austerity cuts which have hit the most vulnerable members of our society the hardest. There's more to come. No bankers have been punished for wrecking the World economy with their greedy pyramid schemes of selling bad debt's which they knew would collapse eventually. In fact, they just keep giving themselves bigger bonuses while we are still paying. I'd say we're pretty entitled to feel angry about that! Let's scale this down a bit to just your personal life. Your boss treats you badly, your partner spends too much of your money, your children are rude, your friends are flaky, and you never seem to have any luck. Are you entitled to feel angry about that? Yes. Are you entitled to BE angry? No. There is a difference between feeling anger, and BEING angry. You are not entitled to be angry. Nobody is. Why? It's destructive. It's a poor strategy for a good life. It makes you miserable, and it means that the people you love are on the receiving end of your constant wrath, even if it's not directed at them. You can stink up the atmosphere like a skunk. That's hard to be around. Stay with me here...solutions are on their way!

Remember earlier I described the man with the muddy filters? I was admiring his jacket, and he was getting ready to kill me because I was looking at him? Here's the problem. He may never know that sometimes people have good intentions. Suppose I had noticed him scowling at me and responded similarly with a scowl of my own. This would simply have confirmed his suspicion that my intention was hostile. He probably assumed I looked away because his snarling was fierce enough to stop me attacking him!

Let's see this principle in action: -

When Daniella was five years old, her Dad walked out. She overheard her Mum talking one day about "another woman". She didn't understand quite what it meant but she believed that her Dad must have hated her to have left like that. Her Mum used to say "It's just you and me now Kid." It was supposed to be comforting, but even though her mum said it to be nice, Daniella could tell there was bitterness in the way she said it. It made her feel uncomfortable, but her Mum was everything to her, and she'd never do anything to upset her. The years went by, and her Mum met a few men who came and went, but Daniella never liked any of them. When Daniella was older, she met Kyle. He was different. He didn't try to control her. He was just laid back, and they started going out. But there was a problem. She still didn't feel very safe. It wasn't rational. She just had this constant feeling that he was going to leave her. She talked to him about it, and he gave her constant reassurance that he loved her, and that everything would be great. One day, she saw Kyle talking to a female workmate on a night out. It all looked just a bit too cosy. The girl was fluttering her eyelashes, and playing with her hair. Later that night Daniella couldn't stand it any longer. She confronted Kyle about his cosy chat. He was flabbergasted. "That was Rachel from the accounts department. She's married and everything". Time went on. Daniella just couldn't shake the feeling. She started calling Kyle more regularly through the day. "I'm just checking you're okay?" she'd say. Kyle started to be a little irritated with her. He tried to hide it, but she could tell. It made her feel even less safe. "Maybe he's up to something" she thought. More time passed, and then Kyle noticed that his emails and texts were being read. He had nothing to hide, but it confirmed his suspicions that Daniella was showing signs of distrust. There was another confrontation. Daniella was almost hysterical. "If you're seeing someone else...just tell me!" Her face was red, and she looked like she wanted to punch him. Kyle remained dumbfounded. Things went steadily downhill from there. Kyle became increasingly unhappy, and eventually, after months of trying to reassure Daniella that all was well, he left. Daniella went back to her mums. Her mum said "Well...It's just you and me now Kid."

The prophecy was fulfilled. It was proven that men never stick around. Another pattern doomed to repeat over and over again. We have to have some empathy here for Daniella. She is a product of her early experiences. Her mum constantly "hypnotised" her with the unwitting suggestion that "It's just you and me. **They** can't be trusted". She imposed her wounding and belief systems on Daniella, and Daniella's subconscious mind has been operating from that hypnotic suggestion ever since. Secretly, even unbeknownst to her herself, her mum never wanted Daniella to ever leave her either. Mum had never had a successful relationship since Daniella's dad had left. **Subconsciously,** she was making sure Daniella never would. That way she could stay in her own anger, pain, and victimhood. Daniella could be proof that they're all ba****ds out there. They could know this together, and that would make it alright. At least they'd have each other. As you'd imagine, Daniella's anger and bitterness towards men merely worsens with every relationship she enters. She starts to date men who she knows will treat her badly. It's what she expects. It's inevitable. We might as well get it over with! The very worst part of this story is that the person with the cynical expectation will only have that World view reinforced. The outcome is as predicted, and the subconscious mind will say "See! I told you they'd let you down!" The belief becomes more fixed and absolute with every event which confirms it.

Now, I know this is a pretty cynical story. Unfortunately, it's also a true one that I have witnessed personally and professionally many times. You will get what you expect, and the subconscious mind will sabotage a situation to ensure that the World fits to your expectations, rather than change your expectations to fit the World. Being angry will just create more situations to be angry about, and a stronger expectation that people will treat you badly.

PUNCHING PILLOWS

Does "venting" anger work? In a word, no! It used to be thought that punching the crap out of a pillow was a good way to release anger. It doesn't work. It might help if you realise how ridiculous you're being, and burst into hysterical laughter at the sight of yourself rolling around on the living room floor with a pillow, but as a serious enterprise, you'll still feel angry, and just a little bit more tired.

Allowing yourself to go into anger is like buying a huge gateau when you're on a diet and expecting yourself to stick to only one slice. It's much better then not to go there in the first place!

42

For all of the reasons we've explored in this chapter, anger is a somewhat insatiable beast when it is simply being vented. I'm sure you know that feeling of being angry and **wanting** to be angrier still. As our sense of entitlement strengthens, as the opioids and adrenaline increase, as our sense of "you're wrong" and "I'm right" gets stronger, the tiger is out of the cage and ready to attack! You're shouting. You're gesticulating, and with each moment the anger becomes stronger and stronger. It's not until you reach a point where you sense that you're about to go **too** far that the "calm down" mechanism kicks in. Sadly, for some, it doesn't, and real damage is done. If that's you, that's even more reason to make sure that you never even let your anger get started! You can't stop yourself from having an angry feeling, but you can take steps to calm it before it gets too big. Whether you are punching pillows, screaming, shouting, breaking things, or being hostile, none of it will help you to feel less angry. It can only enflame further rage, and cause you a whole load of stress which will simply give you more things to be angry about. We need to learn to halt anger before the point of no return is reached, even if it feels good! The final point here is that sometimes anger can be simply a bad habit. While this book is written with full sympathy for anyone finding their anger levels to beyond their control, we must remember that sometimes people are just plain lazy. There's nothing wrong in my opinion with being lazy once in a while. I'm sure it's good for us sometimes, but when it comes to matters of the heart, and positive mental health, complacency is foolhardy. Now, more than ever is the time to motivate. Like I said, this is important.

CHAPTER FOUR – KUNG FU FOCUS!

Eastern philosophical, medicinal, and fighting traditions have a lot to teach us. Shōshin Nagamine, the author of the book *The Essence of Okinawan Karate-Do* said, "Karate may be considered as the conflict within oneself or as a life-long marathon which can be won only through **self-discipline**, hard training, and one's own creative efforts." In both Eastern philosophy and fighting systems there exists the principle of Yin and Yang which is represented by this symbol:-

The Yin Yang symbol shows the nature of duality in wholeness. The circle represents the whole. Within the circle we have the swirling opposites of black and white, soft and hard, penetrative and yielding. The small circle of white in black, and the black in the white represents that these forces are complementary, not opposing, and that one cannot have one without the other. In order to have light for instance, one must also have dark for contrast. When a quality becomes "full" it is said to suddenly become its opposite. As we say, the dark is always its darkest just before the dawn. "Yielding" is the art of using the aggressor's attacking energy to become the very thing which leaves them flat on the floor. All we have to do is get out of the way, and give them a little nudge in the right direction. When done correctly, our opponent will throw themselves to the floor!

Judo is a particularly interesting fighting system from Japan. It is founded on the principles of maximum efficiency/minimum effort, mutual welfare and benefit, and the notion that **softness controls hardness**. It is a defensive system rather than an attacking system. The principle is that when two forces attack each other, head to head, there is explosive energy, like two locomotives crashing head on. The strongest is bound to win. That's just physics. Judo focuses on evading the incoming attack so as to cause the opponent to lose balance, whereupon one could use the weight of the attack against the stronger participant. The potential energy of the attack suddenly becomes its opposite as that force is used simply to destabilise the aggressor. Using this system, "yielding" (getting out of the way) produces better results than attacking, and can result in someone physically smaller and weaker being able to win the battle. In this system, size doesn't matter so much. If you have access to the internet, I'd thoroughly recommend watching some Judo videos to see the process in action.

It's a rather overused cliché but the notion is that of the Peaceful Warrior. This is the person who is entirely capable of looking after him/herself, who needs never to control others or demonstrate their power outwardly. In other words, this is the nicest person you'll ever meet, but he or she will kick your ass if you force them into a confrontation, even if you are bigger than they are. Here, skill is emphasised over strength. This is why we are wise never to mistake kindness for weakness. Those who strut around showing everybody how powerful they are, usually hold very little power internally. Truly powerful people are often softly spoken, and relatively silent.

Kung Fu similarly advocates peace and virtue rather than violence and aggression, while simultaneously working on the development of great power for defence, should it be needed. Although it is primarily a fighting system, it is also a way of life, and a philosophy which focuses on the development of mental and physical discipline as a way to toughen up and meet life's demands gracefully. This is all interesting enough, but one of the reasons I called this chapter Kung Fu Focus, was because central to the presentation of power in Kung Fu is the summoning and channelling of "anger" into a focussed act, usually a punch or a kick. We're all familiar with the sight of Kung Fu masters smashing through planks of wood with a punch. Apparently, this power is wielded through the control and focussing of aggressive energy. Part of the discipline of Kung Fu is learning to tame anger, and then **channel it appropriately** to achieve something.

So, what does all this have to do with your anger? Well, there are two principles here which can provide you with profound insight into how to manage anger effectively. Let's begin by recognising that anger is trying to make a point.

There is a therapeutic principle which says that "All behaviour has a positive intention". What does this mean? It means that your subconscious mind is trying to help you in some way. The problem is that not all of those behaviours are actually helpful. The subconscious mind simply uses the behaviours it currently knows **how** to use. That doesn't necessarily make them the best way to get things done.

What is your anger trying to accomplish? It may seem like some out of control force which has no rhyme or reason, but if you can recognise what really pushes your anger buttons then you're one step closer to solving the problem. If we can figure out what anger is trying to achieve for us, then we can investigate ways of achieving that goal without the undue stress and damage that uncontrolled anger brings with it. Let's look at some examples:-

Behaviour	Subconscious Intention	Outcome
Calling your partner a stupid f*****g idiot.	To encourage your partner to use more foresight before making important decisions.	You feel terrible for insulting your partner, and he or she pretty much hates you!
You are sarcastic with your boss when discussing a new project.	To communicate your frustration over the unreasonable workload you now have to deal with.	Your boss notes your "attitude" problem, and makes a mental note to withdraw a planned promotion.

You put your fist through a window during an argument.	To "win" the dispute with a display of power. To "release" unbearable tension.	Sixteen stitches in your arm. A scar for life. A £330 bill for window replacement.

Sadly, worse things can and do happen. Like I said, anger can cause serious damage. You know that already. So let's take a look at the middle column (intention), using a different format, and suggesting alternative strategies.

Subconscious Intention	Solution	Outcome
To encourage your partner to use more foresight before making important decisions.	Quietly but firmly tell your partner that you are upset by their decision. Explain why.	Maybe they will take your points on board. Maybe they won't. But you stand a much better chance of being "heard" than if you insult them.
To communicate your frustration over the unreasonable workload you now have to deal with.	Ask for a meeting with your boss in private. Air your grievances, and ask if he or she can help you to manage the workload in some way.	Your boss respects your ability to be assertive when necessary. He or she understands your concerns, and enlists other helpers when they are free. They note that you are probably management material.

To "win" the dispute with a display of power. To "release" unbearable tension.	Don't raise your voice. Ask the person you are in dispute with to not raise their voice. When voices are not raised there is no escalation to "unbearable tension". You can display "power" by being the bigger person and refusing to fly into rage. You can use clear communication to resolve the dispute, or agree to disagree, and look for another way to find solution.	No windows are smashed. You stand a good chance of resolving the dispute amicably. You are learning to be a person of power successfully controlling anger and channelling your messages appropriately.

I do understand of course that in real life, many situations cannot be pigeon-holed quite as neatly as we see here, but the principle remains true. Anger has an agenda. It is trying to achieve something for you. If we can understand what the agenda is, we can make sure that we learn the skills necessary to teach the subconscious mind that the anger behaviour, well-intended as it may be, is not helping. We get much better results when we "yield" and approach softly.

CHANNELLING ANGER APPROPRIATELY

You will remember I made the point that feeling angry is different from **being** angry? This may at first glance appear to be mere wordplay, but there's more going on here than meets the eye. If anger has an agenda, and our job is to have that agenda met without the use of violence and rage, then it should make sense that **being angry is unconducive to getting what you need.** If we embody anger as a state of being, we have already begun to lose control. We are then being driven by irrational instinctive limbic system impulses, which while strong for physical fights, remain weak when it comes to rational resolution of problems. How many satisfactory results have ever been delivered for you by **being** angry? Not many I'll bet! But, when you are able to **feel** anger without "becoming" angry, then you are able to put that feeling of anger to good use because a) you're not being flooded by an overwhelming rush of chemical stimulation and uncontrollable emotion, and b) you still have access to your logical brain as a result. In short, you can still think, and when you can still think you have a much greater chance of actually making the point you wish to make, or getting what you want or need.

Now, let's go back to our image of the Kung-Fu master smashing through a plank of wood with his fist. If the Kung-Fu master loses his temper, he will also lose his focus. He may start pummelling the wood in sheer frustration. Every blow will be wasted. He simply cannot generate the energy necessary to deliver the focussed power needed to break through while he is not in control. What you see with our Kung-Fu master is someone demonstrating great concentration, poise, and calm. The Kung-Fu master is summoning the necessary energy into a single focussed point. When he is ready he unleashes that energy with full force, but he remains controlled throughout. Only with this focussed control can he achieve his goal.

It's just an image, and although in a way it advocates violent and explosive force, not really suitable for settling disputes, the point here is to understand the principle. If anger is an attempt to be powerful, then we don't achieve it with an unfocussed display of rage, coupled with a loss of control. This may have the effect of intimidating an opponent, but it definitely won't ultimately lead to you getting what you want, or being heard in any positive way. Your adversary might do as you wish because they fear your rage, but that's just a plain ugly situation. They'll resent you too. No satisfaction can come from that. What you really want is for them to **want** to help you to get what you want or need; willingly, or better still, lovingly.

You need to understand something. Most of the time, people want to help each other out. This might be news to you, but remember what we said about self-fulfilling prophecy earlier? If your perception is that people are generally hostile, you will act as though this is true. You will attack as a form of defence, and you will find that your adversary will attack back for the same reason. The situation will quickly escalate. The crazy thing about this dynamic is that neither of you will even be fighting about what you are fighting about at this point! You'll simply be fighting to "win". When that means crushing your opponent, or them crushing you, or you crushing each other, the outcome is not going to be favourable for anyone. Even if you win, you lose!

We achieve power with calm focussed action. This is what is meant by channelling anger appropriately. The goal is to be heard, or receive what's fair for you, or to change a situation which is causing you stress, without violence or harm.

SOFTNESS CONTROLS HARDNESS

Pretty much everyone who consults with a therapist brings scepticism, suspicion, some resentment, and a little bit of anger to their first consultation. They are angry because they have a difficulty that they haven't managed to tackle on their own. We like to be in control of our own destinies. All therapists have to manage this (veiled) hostility because it's the messenger who gets shot. Initially, the therapist is the visible face of a loss of control for the person presenting with a problem. The therapist is a reminder of (self-perceived) failure, and a blank canvas upon which to project that anger. At least that's what's going on subconsciously.

So how do we handle this? The short answer is that we approach our new client with "softness". Sometimes their passive-aggressive (we'll talk about this shortly) feelings will leak out, either in direct challenges to our counsel, or in subtle body language changes. However it presents, it's still a challenge. As a therapist we **expect** this. **It's nothing personal.** We begin by recognising that the anger which is being unfairly directed towards us is actually not about us. Furthermore, we learn to look beyond the anger, to the person behind it. People are not their anxieties, or their depression, or their anger. People are generally rather nice beings. You just have to expect to find that **before** you'll see it! So, I just simply "let" people be angry for a while. I make space for their scepticism and suspicion. I don't take it personally. I'd be exactly the same in their shoes. The outcome of this is that there's no hint of attack towards them in my manner. In other words, I'm not acting defensively. I'm not repressing or hiding dislike or hostility. It's genuinely not present. They are totally allowed to be sceptical, cynical, suspicious, and cheesed off that they are in my consulting room. I have genuine empathy for them because they are in pain. It may be being projected on to me, but it's not about me. Why would I take it personally?

Now, imagine going through life with this attitude.

What if you were to recognise that when people display anger or hostility, it's often because they are feeling stressed about things which have little or nothing to do with you?

You might be the person who receives it, but that's probably just because you happen to be in the wrong place at the wrong time. Then your filters wouldn't create a picture of someone displaying hostile behaviour as being hostile because of you, or towards you. You'd simply see someone who's stressed out. Then, instead of feeling like you're being attacked, you could respond differently. When we respond with softness, usually, something amazing happens.

The energy of hatred suddenly becomes its opposite.

Let's think about this for a moment. This is a true story. About six months ago, on a Saturday, I was sitting in a café in Bristol at lunch time. Outside, two guys who had clearly been drinking alcohol started kicking off at each other. Voices were raised, and it was starting to cause quite a scene. Then the pushing started. Seconds later, one of the men pulled his arm back and took the biggest swing. It was a big punch, but the other guy saw it coming and pulled back, causing the man to literally swing himself round in a circle as the punch fell into thin air. Instead of jumping in on the attack, which with the aggressor clearly off balance would have been devastating, the defending man simply stepped back. There was a stand-off for a moment, and then there were a few words exchanged which I couldn't hear, and literally seconds later they were hugging each other. Not awkward hugs, but great big loving hugs. They were both smiling. The defending man put his arm around the fellow, and they walked away chatting. It's one of those really strange things about men that many women cannot fathom at all! Men can often do this. Not always, but often. Once the energy is released, equilibrium is quickly restored, and love follows. Male friends who fight, fight it out first, and then hug it out fast. I've certainly experienced it. If you're male and reading this you may know exactly what I'm talking about? This is an extreme example of the principle in action, and it actually came to physical fisticuffs here, but the same mechanism can work without fisticuffs too. What we are seeing is the energy of hatred and anger suddenly becoming softness and love. It's a weird phenomenon, but it's what can happen.

Now, take that same idea and apply it to a different angry situation. Let's suppose you've come home from work really tired. All you want to do is switch off. You literally don't even want to think about anything. Your brain is exhausted. Your wife has other ideas. She's been trying to book a holiday, and she's dragged you in to help out with a friend's wedding. Normally, you'd be fine with this, but today everything went wrong. You've had enough. You sit seething as she starts to reel off a list of things she's got lined up for you to do on Saturday, until you just can't hold it in for a single moment more. "WILL YOU SHUT THE F*** UP WOMAN! YOU NEVER F*****G STOP DO YOU?!" What happens next will be crucial. If she takes this personally (it certainly sounds it doesn't it?) there will be a fast escalation and they'll soon be fighting about how she spent all day finding the right holiday, how he's such an "ungrateful ba****d", and who didn't do what last week. If however, she is soft, and she looks beyond the insult to see the person beyond the anger, she'll see something else. She might then say, "What's up? I can see you're really stressed. Did something happen today?" Then they could be having a whole different conversation. He'll say immediately "I'm sorry! That was totally out of order. It was just one of the days where everything went pear shaped. First I got stuck in traffic....."

Softness controls hardness.

PASSIVE–AGGRESSIVE IS NOT SOFTNESS

Passive-Aggressive is a term used to describe hostility which is disguised as passivity. You might remember in our earlier case studies that when Karen asked Pete to pick up his wet towels, he took offence and actually became less helpful. This is a good example of passive-aggressive behaviour. It's not outright. It's passive on the surface but seething underneath. It's important that we don't get passive-aggressive behaviour and softness mixed up. They're definitely not the same thing.

Experts disagree on the exact figure, but we do know that a large proportion of our communications with each other are non-verbal. It's not so much what you say, as how you say it. This includes your body language, facial expressions, tone of voice, and subsequent behaviours. One of the ways that we can communicate hostility is by being deliberately obstructive while trying to appear helpful. We might do as we're asked but purposely do a poor job of it. We might be deliberately late to a meeting, or we might just sulk and stink up the atmosphere. "Fine" doesn't always mean fine.

When I was doing my Cognitive Behavioural Therapy training, we were given a list of passive-aggressive traits. As we read through them, we had a good laugh between ourselves because to most points we were all nodding and saying "Yep...that's me!" It's worth understanding then that it's close to impossible to not be passive-aggressive sometimes. We are, as we explored in the beginning of the book, all placed in situations where we need to remain polite and compliant when really we'd like to throttle the awkward fool who is making life unnecessarily difficult for us. Our lives often require that we deal with people who we wouldn't choose to spend time with in any other situation. There's a certain amount of inevitability therefore that we will have to bite our tongues often, and smile sweetly. That's just life! When you're less angry generally, you'll be able to cope with these situations gracefully by learning not to take it personally!

However, passive-aggressive behaviour with people you have a personal relationship with is going to do damage. Playing mind-games, that is, having an agenda to "win" without admitting that there's a battle being waged, is going to make life extremely complicated for you because it will set you up with an adversarial outlook. It's only a short hop from there to paranoia. If you're acting sweetly, and harbouring hostility, then it will be easy to assume that everyone else harbours hostility secretly too. You get what you expect remember? That's going to make the whole World seem hostile and lead you right back to square one. So let's be clear that even if you are a master of mind games, passive-aggressive approaches are no victory at all because you'll still have an opponent, and that will mean there is still a need for defence, which will create attack. Softness is a state of mind. Don't confuse sarcasm, obstruction, and mind games for softness. They are not the same thing.

Summary

Here's what we've learned so far: -

* Generally high stress levels are a common cause of anger. Even normally mild people can find themselves acting angrily when their emotional arousal levels are high. When this is the case there are few deeply rooted problems to resolve. It's just a case of reducing stress generally, and normal service will resume quite naturally. A certain degree of anger repression is inevitable but repressing anger when stress levels are too high can cause the pressure cooker to explode.

* When anger is chronic, regardless of external pressures, there is almost certainly a reason for it. This can include wounding in early life, leading to anger as a defence mechanism against events which either frighten you, or threaten to cause you to re-experience hurt and/or powerlessness from the past. Attack is a form of defence, and the subconscious mind can become hyper-vigilant to the presence of anything which might constitute a threat in this regard. The outcome of this is that it doesn't take much for your brain to see threat where none is intended. When anger is triggered by these defensive mechanisms, it's next to impossible to retain control because your brain favours an instinctive response to a thoughtful one when faced with danger, and your intellect is temporarily overwhelmed by the signals from your emotional brain, the limbic system. This is one potential reason that you haven't yet been able to control your anger.

* Negative experiences from the past are imprinted in your subconscious mind causing you to expect more of the same in the future. This occurs because your mind filters reality according to what it expects to find. The subconscious mind will delete information which does not meet with your expectation, and at the same time will seize upon, and inflate the information which does. Therefore, when someone is nice, you assume that there must be an ulterior motive instead of understanding that some people are just nice because nice makes the World go round more smoothly.

* Expecting to find the worst in life operates as a self-fulfilling prophecy. When you approach situations and people with an expectation that they will be hostile towards you, you unwittingly put out a defensive signal of hostility which makes people want to distance themselves from you. Thus, you rarely find the best in people, or situations, and the outcomes are not positive. Then, your brain accepts this as confirmation that your original assessment was correct, leading to a strengthening of the belief system that the World is hostile, and that there's something fundamentally wrong with you, causing more of the same in future.

* As a result of these expectations, it's not at all uncommon for angry people to become "controlling". This is an effort to retain complete control over the person or situation in order to ensure that the worst cannot be allowed to happen. People and situations generally do not respond positively to people controlling them too tightly, and once again the prophecy is fulfilled when the situation explodes, or the person leaves.

* You become angry when your "rules" are being broken. When something is considered as a "must'" or a "should", disappointment and irritation will naturally follow when something doesn't happen the way you want it to. This can be moral, but just as often it's simply because we believe that certain things should be done a certain way.

* Anger can be psychologically and physically addictive. Powerful habit forming drugs usually reserved for emergency situations can be released into the bloodstream when we become angered, and the accompanying sense of power can feel really good in the moment. Unfortunately, it

invariably ends in damage being caused in some way, and thus ultimately, regret.

* In addition to this, the feeling of being "right" and making someone else "wrong", can also feel really good, especially if your personal history has been one of continued disempowerment. If you've had a lifetime of people telling you that you're not good enough, then it feels pretty good to be the one who's in control of the situation for once. This is the root of bullying. Even if you are correct in your assessment of the situation, no good can come of this because it will move quickly from trying to be heard, to assuming power over another. The power is temporary and the results are usually catastrophic.

* We become angry when someone takes something we don't wish to give, or dumps something on us which we don't wish to receive.

* Anger is difficult to quell because it comes laden with a great big dollop of self-righteousness and entitlement. When you're in the right, and the other is in the wrong, it's a pretty great opportunity to get that power fix and feel justified about it. This is a **strong** pull!

* Sometimes we're creating anger for ourselves with little justification. This is because we are choosing to interpret events in a way which does all of the above!

* We know that losing your temper doesn't usually stem anger. Once could assume that "venting" in some way would "release" the angry energy. There are some situations where this could happen, but for the most part allowing anger to take over will just make you feel more anger. Smashing your TV to smithereens because the remote isn't working is not going to make you feel any better. You'll feel just as angry, but you'll have a new expense and a nice topping of embarrassment and self-loathing to go with it. It's better to just not go there in the first place.

* Anger has an agenda. It is basically trying to protect you. If we can identify the agenda, then we can implement strategies which will achieve that goal without the unnecessary carnage which accompanies **uncontrolled** anger.

* Softness is more powerful than Hardness. By learning to "yield", that is to step out of the way of a perceived attack, we leave our opponent unbalanced and vulnerable while maintaining our own dignity and poise. Then, we retain intellectual control, and our composure will serve us in reaching the desired goal.

* We need to understand that softness is not repressing or hiding our anger. Nor is it playing mind games, or becoming the King or Queen of sarcasm. Softness is **appropriate** action.

* And, finally, I left this point until last because it leads us nicely to where we want to go. Anger can have great positive power. When we can learn to tame anger and channel it appropriately, it can move mountains! In fact, we need it, and I'm all for it, but it should only ever be brought to the fights which we really need to have. Anything else will be destructive and energy zapping for you and everyone involved.

CHAPTER FIVE – MOVING FROM RAGE TO GRACE

So, you now have a deep understanding of the mechanics of anger. The next thing for you to do is to figure out which of these mechanisms is responsible for the largest part of your anger. In the rest of the book, I'm going to take the summary above and provide meaningful solutions to each of these anger-producing problems. You will need to implement the ones which you feel apply to your own life.

STRESS

Well, this is a big subject which I tackle in full detail in my debut book "You Can Fix Your Anxiety – A Power Guide To Eliminating Stress, Anxiety And Depression". If you'd like further in-depth information on how to tackle stress and anxiety properly, please do take a look at You Can Fix Your Anxiety. It's available in paperback and Kindle formats from Amazon on this link: -

http://amzn.to/1qCFnLu

There's not room for such a deep analysis here, so I will just keep the focus on a few fast and effective areas in which you can make things better right away.

Stress is what happens when the demands placed upon you appear to exceed your ability to cope. Every time you feel overwhelmed, it creates stress, and stress accumulates. In the opening to this book I explained how the limbic system can become overly aroused by the presence of threat. What this means in practice is that there is too much stress being generated on a day to day basis, and the animal brain is responding to that stress with one of the three main responses; anxiety, depression, or anger. You will remember that we were looking at the way stress can accumulate in the nervous system, leading potentially to a blowout. I said:-

"The rule is that where there is emotional arousal, there must also be discharge of that energy".

What we need is some way of reversing that accumulation of pressure **before** it reaches breaking point. One of the solutions to this overload of **arousal** is to practice regular relaxation. This is a form of **discharge** for that energy. Now before you decide that this won't work for you, let me assure you that it absolutely will! Think of the limbic system as an engine. When an engine becomes overheated, it blows a gasket, right? Well, this is just the same. Relaxation is to the limbic system what switching the overheated engine off is to a car. It literally "cools" the entire system. If you keep running the car when there's no cooling, it's going to blow at some point. If you let it cool down, it will stay cool.

By reducing the amount of stress and tension that goes into a stress bucket on a daily basis we can de-arouse (calm) the limbic system and return control to the frontal lobe. To this end I am now including for you a relaxation recording to use. This particular recording is more than just a relaxation however. This particular recording is built with anger management in mind. You can use this recording whenever you are drifting off to sleep. It will be very useful for those people who struggle to get to sleep, particularly if you have a very busy mind and have difficulty switching off at bedtime. It's absolutely fine if you are listening to the recording and fall asleep midway. Countless clients have reported this. The effect of this will be that you will have a deeper and more restful sleep, since your mind will be quiet as you make that transition from waking to sleep.

This recording can also be used during the daytime. It doesn't matter whether your mind drifts or doesn't drift. In other words you may be completely aware of all the words of the recording throughout, but just as often, you may find that your mind drifts off, and you wonder what you've been thinking about for the last 30 minutes while the recording has been playing. Either way is fine. The specific suggestions will help, but the relaxation will help too, so it's all good! This deep relaxation process is very healthy for your mind and body. This is the kind of relaxation which will settle your limbic system. When you use this recording regularly, you can think of it as a cumulative positive effect. You will notice that there are direct hypnotic suggestions involved. The idea with these is that these suggestions will take root in your mind and become **automatic** instructions for times of stress and anger, allowing you to **respond rather**

than react. Response is thoughtful and deliberate, while reaction is automatic, and often ill-considered. We want response, not reaction.

So you should experience a natural decrease in the intensity of angry thoughts and feelings and also in the regularity of those angry thoughts and feelings. The recording is housed on a private page of my website and you will need a password to access it. Enter the following as you see it

Here's the link: - https://bit.ly/2SjY7xq

Password: **releaseanger**

Other considerations when it comes to stress must also include your current circumstances. I don't mind sharing with you that I don't much like the pace of the World these days. It's fast, frenetic, pressured, sometimes unfair, and often quite ruthless. If I had it my way, we'd all be sitting on a beach sipping Margherita's right now! It goes without say that we are all doing what we have to do to get by, and that there are some circumstances which are difficult or impossible to change immediately. Where that's the case, so be it, for now. However, quite often we are unnecessarily enduring circumstances which are deeply upsetting to us in some way, and the question needs to be asked then whether it is actually within our power to make some changes?

Human beings are often held back by insecurities and fears which cause us to settle for an arrangement which really isn't working for us because we're too afraid of change and uncertainty. We know that the subconscious mind doesn't like change. It prefers the devil it knows. If you are enduring circumstances which are deeply unsatisfactory for you though, and finding that you have uncontrollable anger, then you can be pretty sure that your anger is trying to get your attention!

The subconscious mind can and does create emotional responses to let us know when something is not working. It's entirely possible that your anger is a direct response from your deeper self to these unsatisfactory circumstances. I know that there is an irony in this. On the one hand the mind wants the devil it knows, and on the other, it's screaming for change. Unfortunately, this is how the subconscious mind works on occasion. It is trying to have simultaneous needs met, and sometimes those needs come

61

into conflict with each other. So I'll settle this one for you. The need to have certainty is a constant, as far as the subconscious mind is concerned. It always has that agenda. The need for change is almost certainly more pressing at this moment (assuming you recognise deeply unsatisfactory circumstances). Uncertainty may be uncomfortable, but ignoring the need for change can have much more negative effects, such as anxiety, depression, burnout, and rage. Burying ones head in the sand rarely pays off. We need to be courageous in identifying what isn't working, and opting for something which will. That's going to be work, but so goes the old saying "A change is as good as a rest". If we can recognise that resistance to change is to be expected, and factor in some tolerance to that inevitable discomfort without being **steered** by it, we'll find that the pain of change is temporary, while the benefits of resolving our untenable circumstances are significant. It's not a perfect solution I know, but it's what grit and determination demand. If you're finding that you're stressed out all the time, I really would encourage you to have a good look at your circumstances and ask whether you need change, and take seriously the notion that change may not only be possible, but may also be vital for your wellbeing.

In addition to taking time to relax your limbic system and build a less stressful lifestyle wherever possible, we also need to be aware of the potentially negative effects of using alarming language and negative imagination when processing our view of the world. In the same way that negative interpretational styles can create anger, they can also create stress and anxiety. The imagination sees very little difference between what is imagined, and what is real. Let me explain.

Suppose I become convinced that while I am out at work, my wife is nipping over to the neighbours for some extra marital excitement. I have no evidence exactly, but I have some suspicions. Then my mind starts to make up stories. Soon, I'm picturing them in bed together. In days, I go from calm and placid, to full of rage and grief. It turns out that I genuinely had the whole thing all wrong. She did go over to his house a couple of times, but then I found out she's been planning me a surprise birthday garden party and he's been helping with the arrangements and setup. Silly me! But, the fact that my information was inaccurate made no difference to my limbic system. So, when it comes to the generating of negative emotional arousal, it doesn't matter whether something is true or not, it only matters that it is **believed** to be true! That's all a limbic system needs to work us into a state of high agitation.

Take this understanding as it applies to anger, and now think about how this same principle can make a person hugely and unnecessarily stressed or anxious. The more we fret about the outcomes of situations using negative forecasting, the more our limbic system brain will be forced to respond with evasive responses like anxiety and depression. So, be careful about the kind of ruminations you entertain in your mind. A famous Zen quote goes something like "Many visitors will pass through your house. Just don't invite them all to sit and have tea with you." The antidote to these negative imaginings and thoughts is not to fight with them, but instead to accept them as they pass through your mind without agreeing to entertain them as valid and important. The mind produces a certain amount of "noise" in its everyday functioning. We need to recognise it for what it is, but it is true that these difficulties are persistent for some people. Reducing your level of overall arousal using relaxation techniques, and changing untenable circumstances will help, but beyond this, it is also necessary to practice good mental hygiene. That means deliberately focussing on how things could go right, instead of constantly imagining what might go wrong. Stress and anxiety, I'm afraid, is my other book, but if you can consider these important points you'll be pointing in the right direction.

HEALING THE PAST

We discussed anger as a defensive mechanism against being afraid, and then against being hurt. For both of these threats we are going to need an effective strategy to make sure that we are protected. When you feel protected, there will literally be no reason for the anger to be triggered.

So, let's go back to our earlier examples from the beginning of Chapter Two. Remember James? His parents had that awful row and he's particularly sensitive to anything connected with the theme of lying. He gets really angry when people lie to him and he just loses it if anyone accuses him of doing so. His underlying belief system is sustained with the formula **"When people don't tell the truth, very bad things happen!"**

This is a kind of algebraic formula. It's like when A happens, B is the result. It's <u>subconscious,</u> so James doesn't even know why he feels these feelings. He just does. Next we have Pete. As you may remember Pete grew up feeling constant disappointment as he sought his parents' attention and approval. He thought he was over it, but it comes back to haunt him in his romantic relationships.

In both of these cases there is a very important ingredient necessary to overcoming this anger; in a word, **healing.** This is unfinished business as far as the subconscious mind is concerned. So let's break that down, and understand what this word really means in this context. First of all, James is wounded. It is that simple. There's no other way of putting it. He has sustained a wound and it has not yet healed. In a way, James is stuck in time. More accurately, we could say that a "part" of James is stuck in time. We all know how those peak experiences in our lives are etched into our memories quite vividly, and it's the six year old James who is stuck. This is because the brain attributes significance to these moments and stores them permanently, freezing the moment of trauma in the memory banks. Unfortunately, not only is the memory itself stored, but alongside that, all of the assumptions and feelings which went with that memory. When a memory is made in early life, very often the assumptions and interpretations of what those events mean can be quite inaccurate by adult standards. The shock remains, and metaphorically, a frame is placed around that memory with a big sign underneath in red letters saying "This must never happen again!" So, time passes, James grows up, and everything about him changes. Everything that is, except that one vitally important piece of information, that lying leads to terrible things. That stays the same, burned into his subconscious memory banks vividly and unshakably. It's so much a part of James at this point that it's never even questioned. It's just "the way things are". Now, any one of us might agree with the basic proposal. It's true that largely, lying is not a good way to live life, but for James this belief creates massive over-reaction.

So, here's what **healing** will mean for him. James will need to "unfreeze" that moment. It's hanging there on the wall, in the memory databanks. Somehow James is going to need to take the picture off the wall and inspect it. I'm going to explain shortly how to do this effectively, but for now, just stay with me on the metaphor.

THIS MUST NEVER HAPPEN AGAIN!

The subconscious mind has been avoiding this material. In fact, it's been engineering around it since it happened, so it's not going to happen all by itself. James will need to make a conscious decision to locate the picture and engage with it. As he takes the picture off the wall, it comes to life. He watches his father scream at his mother and he sees a six year old James looking terrified. And, in that moment, he realises something deeply. This is what it's all been about. All these years of over-reacting to lies, is because of this one moment. But, he's watching with **adult** eyes now. He can understand much more clearly what's happening here. He stops the movie, and imagines stepping into the picture. He sits with young James, puts an arm around his shoulder, and says "Hey Buddy. I'm really sorry you had to see that. I know it really scared you." Young James loosens up a bit. "Is Dad leaving?" he says. "No...Dad's not leaving". Young James visibly relaxes. "Sometimes people just say and do things in the heat of the moment. It looks really bad, but most of the time it's not as bad as it seems. They just have some problems that they need to work out together". Young James continues to look perplexed. "I know that you think that this is all about someone lying, but actually Mum and Dad have been really worried about lots of things and that's why they're fighting. It doesn't mean they don't love each other". Young James looks up, looking relieved. James continues "I'll tell you what. If you are ever feeling scared again, just call for me, and I'll come back and sit with you again. Any time! How would that be?" Young James looks much brighter. "Yes. OK!" "So, you're okay now?" "Yes, I'm feeling better!" James hangs the picture back on the hook.

Now, let's have a look at Pete. This is a slightly different case. The wounding is deeper, and in some ways less easily resolved, because Pete isn't merely labouring under a simple misunderstanding. Pete has been repeatedly sent the message that he's not good enough. It doesn't matter whether that message was sent deliberately or inadvertently. It still affected his sense of self-worth deeply. This has left Pete with a very sore button, and like James, he also has a picture in the gallery with the same red words. Pete has also spent his entire life **engineering** around his wounding. He's chosen friends who don't challenge him, he's quit jobs that did, and woe betide anyone who might dare to offer constructive criticism.

He has found ways to explain his behaviour with other rationalisations though. Intellectually, he says he's over it. "That's all in the past. I don't have much to do with my parents anymore so I don't have to worry about it". He says "I just don't suffer fools gladly". He's brave, but he's also misinformed because actually this wound is not about his parents, or anyone else for that matter. It's about him. His upbringing may have been the cause of the problem, but ultimately it remains **his** problem because it exists only in **his** mind and heart. His parents could die and it would still be there. Nobody else can fix it. It is his cross to bear...or to heal. So, what is healing in this context?

First of all, Pete needs to come to an understanding of the source of his anger. Picture this. Young Pete sees his Mum coming down the street with shopping bags. His heart truly sinks because she's coming home. Whose fault is that? Is the boy a nasty little runt for being so heartless? Or, has the Mother given the boy some reason to feel that way towards her? I get that there are plenty of children who go wayward for all sorts of complex reasons, who develop anger towards their parents, or other figures in their lives, sometimes for no good reason. As a pure example though, I'd have to say that nine times out of ten, that's the parents' doing. It has been wisely said that people forget what you said to them, but they always remember how you made them feel. James is a child. He doesn't possess the complicated adult ability to temper his feelings with rationality. He just knows how she makes him feel, and it's certainly not wanted, loved, or valued. That sinking feeling in his heart is anything but. So, now, adult James is finally connecting with the truth of this. He's finally allowing himself to fully feel the pain of what could have been...what **should** have been. It's a tragedy really. As the tears stream down James' face he starts to understand something deeply. He finally gets it. He knows...I mean REALLY knows, that they let him down. He finally understands that they should have done better. This is a pretty awful truth to face for a number of reasons. First of all, it's deeply engrained in each of us to feel a sense of protectiveness towards our parents. This is genetic, biological, evolutionary, and culturally encouraged. Family is family. You stick together. Secondly, admitting that family actually didn't stick together is painful. There has been a failure of duty, and that hurts. Thirdly, it's very difficult to shake the feeling that it's your fault. Children process reality with themselves firmly in the centre. In other words, when you are a child everything is about "me". The logic of a child is that if mum and dad aren't showing adequate caring, then it must be **my** fault. The only logical conclusion then that one can arrive at is that **I** must be flawed, unwanted, disliked, not good enough, bad, and ultimately...unlovable. When you understand this, you can see what a complicated bundle of emotions there are to unravel, and you can quickly see why there is such resistance to dealing with the issue. There's no doubt about it. There's going to be pain and disappointment in processing this. But, the question has to be asked. "Is this burden really mine to carry for the rest of my life?" Indeed, with it, a proper life is out of reach. How can you love and be loved with a faulty belief system like this accompanying you everywhere you go?

There's only one way to process this fully, and that's through the emotion of grief. Grief for what could have been, what should have been, grief for the fact that they let you down, grief for the fact that the World is a cruel place at times, and grief for all the pain you've suffered and time you've wasted beating yourself up for something which was never about you in the first place. It was always about them. This is a big ask of Pete. He's always been a fighter. He's had to be. Letting his guard down doesn't come easy, but Pete needs to know that not all battles are fought with fists. Some are fought with gentleness, and when softness doesn't come easily, then allowing yourself to connect with this is an act of real power and courage. This is how Pete meets with his healing. This is an over-simplified version for the purposes of clear explanation, but the essence of it is what must happen.

Now let me explain what's happening in these examples. There is a lot going on. Hopefully, by now, you understand that the subconscious mind sticks to its existing beliefs and edits out anything which doesn't agree with its pre-supposed world view. Healing then, is not simply a good cry and an epiphany of understanding, though these are often valuable components of the healing process. To my mind, central to the healing process is the re-writing of belief systems at the core level. Where is the core level? Well, it's in the brain, but it's also in the heart. In order for something to be **known** as true, it must also be **felt** to be true. Rational explanation alone is not sufficient to create this kind of change. That is why you can't talk yourself out of having angry responses. The change must happen in the heart too. Now, if we look at the above examples we see that in both cases we succeed in presenting a case which is not only understood to be true but can also be FELT to be true because the evidence is ultimately undeniable. We finally see it with our own eyes. Why didn't we see it before? Well, because we weren't looking in the right place, and we weren't looking with the right eyes. Like I said, the picture must be consciously lifted and interacted with for change to occur, and then we have to know what we're doing, and why we're doing it. When you successfully re-write the core belief, then there is literally no trigger left to cause the anger. I am not speaking figuratively. There is **literally** no trigger. At one level, it's a mechanical matter. If you take the spanner out of the works, the gears can operate smoothly again.

So, with James, we help his inner being, child, self, template of experience, stuck-in-time-ness, call it what you will, to review the situation with fresh eyes. Then, he was able to soften the shock that his younger self was feeling, which made the template much less likely to react violently to any perceived slights against that wounded place. We left Young James smiling and relaxed. He'll stay that way because we also changed his beliefs. He no longer sees it as his job to make sure that "this must never happen again". With the re-write, he survives the experience. Not only that, he also receives a massive dose of positive attention, and makes a new friend. Who is that? His new friend is himself. We have completely altered the dynamics of the situation. He's no longer at war with himself, or the World.

You will notice that everything in that example is presented in **present** tense. This is absolutely deliberate. With hypnotherapy we use methods of "regression" to ask the person to travel, in their minds eye, back in time to the origin of their problem. Once they are there, they are in the past, but experiencing it as the present. It is from this point that the problem can be properly addressed. The mind stores its information chronologically (in time order). It's no good trying to fix something that happened years ago while you're twenty years in the future. The two areas of the mind aren't fully connecting. We need to find the spot in the brain where the memory resides and meet it there. This is not literal. I'm not a neuro-wizard. The point is metaphorical, but that is exactly why this method works. The brain is metaphorical too. It can handle the idea of imaginarily travelling back in time to fix a faulty template, or travelling to the exact spot in the brain where that memory is stored. You just have to use the right setting and language to facilitate the process.

Though I wasn't explicit about how we helped Pete, we used a similar process to have him revisit his younger self. His grieving, and ultimate realisation that he wasn't unlovable at all, but was in fact let down by the people who were supposed to nurture him fully was what changed the way that he feels. Either willingly, or unwittingly, he was sent the erroneous message that he wasn't good enough because they were too selfish, wounded, or bitter to give him what he needed. He can still have empathy for them. This is not about marking his parents up as rotten people. If they were, that's fine, but often they only behave the way they behave because they are wounded too, or simply didn't know how to be good parents. It doesn't excuse it, but at least Pete understands the truth of the situation now. Pete has to heal his **own** wounds. The goal is not make a victim of oneself, but to recognise head-on that the error was not his, and that he is not unworthy. His healing follows the same principles. By seeing for himself, with his own eyes, maybe for the first time ever, that it really wasn't him that was unworthy, he was able to experience a complete re-writing of that erroneous belief he's been carrying around. The real magic of this is that it becomes not only an intellectual understanding, but because the truth of it is so evident at that point, it also becomes felt understanding. In other words, there is a change of heart as well as a change of mind. Again, the outcome is that there is literally no trigger left.

The outcome of this is very truly that both James and Pete experience a huge reduction in their anger levels. The "reason" for the anger literally no longer exists. It has been re-written, and transformed.

TRANSFORMATION

I have been a therapist using these methods successfully for the last thirteen years, and I can promise you with my hand on my heart that I have seen many people undergo amazing transformations with these simple but profound approaches. I have also seen my fair share of complications. The examples given above are text book examples. Everything is neat and tidy. I deliberately designed them that way to illustrate some points. However, we know that life isn't always quite to plan.

In a moment I'm going to describe two simple methods that most people will be able to use at home to shift perspective on their past wounding. Before I do though, I have to explain the limitations of self-help. Your situation may be much more complex than those illustrated by James and Pete. My primary motivation for explaining these processes here was to illustrate the mechanisms by which healing **can** occur, but it is beyond the scope of this book to facilitate these processes to the same depth that one would expect in a true one on one therapeutic setting. If you would like to explore these processes fully, my advice would be to visit a professional therapist with the appropriate skills. Then you would have the support and guidance necessary to work through any complications which could arise, and you would have a framework of safety to ensure that your outcomes remain positive. With that understood, I am going to offer a diluted version of the first process which should be quite safe to use on a self-help basis. If for any reason these exercises make you feel uncomfortable in any way, please discontinue use immediately. Here's how you do it: -

* Sit quietly in an undisturbed space and bring your attention to your breath. Your mind will wander. Thoughts will arise. Just notice them without attaching any great significance to them. If you experience a distracted mind telling you to go and do something else, just notice it, and then let it go. If you lose focus, remain relaxed, and simply bring your attention back to your breath. Do this for about five or ten minutes. You will feel your body relaxing and with enough time and patience you should notice a sense of peace develop. This is basic meditation. It just helps us to slow the mind down, and find a space where we can think and

focus more clearly, as well as have a deeper connection to our internal world.

* When you feel focused, just think about the last time you felt really angry. You will probably start to feel that feeling again as you remember it. Locate the feeling. Is it in your head, your chest, your belly, or somewhere else?

* Once you have located the feeling, take your attention to the feeling and imagine sitting with it like a friend. Be "curious" about the feeling. Notice whether it has a shape, a colour, or a texture. Is it large or small, heavy or light, dark or bright, or is just a sensation? As you locate it you will notice that it comes into clearer focus. Just continue to sit with it without fear or frustration. Just be present.

* Then, with that curiosity, just ask the question in your mind "What emotion sits behind this anger?" Don't try to force an answer. Just be patient and wait. If your subconscious mind is ready to reveal this to you, it will. If it isn't then it won't. Just notice whether there is sadness or anxiety behind the anger. If it's sadness, then it's probably about being hurt. If it's anxiety, then it's probably about being afraid.

* Imagine then sending from your heart as much love as you can towards that place in your body that feels angry/anxious/hurt. Be really genuine with this. Do it for as long as it feels real, and as long as it feels pleasurable. You should notice your anger either softens, melts, or disappears.

* If it feels appropriate you can add worded messages as you send this love. You can say "I know you've been feeling really angry. I'm sorry you got hurt/were afraid. I will do my best to keep you safe now". Do this for as long as it feels sincere and healing.

* When you are ready, gently disengage from those feelings, take a few moments to centre yourself by focusing on your breath once again, and then slowly bring yourself back to ordinary awareness and open your eyes, feeling good.

Don't attempt to go any deeper than this without supervision. If you stick to the programme you should experience a significant shift towards feeling calmer and more supported. As I said, if it's not working for you, then discontinue use. For most people though, this will help. What you are doing here is sending support to the angry part of yourself in a way which will make him/her feel much safer. If you've been following the logic, the safer you feel, the less likely you are to respond with anger in life. For that reason you should think of this as a **daily practice**. Providing that you are comfortable with the approach, a few minutes of this practice a day may really help you to feel heard, understood, and supported at a very deep level. It's simple. Keep it that way. The effects will be cumulative. It can be profoundly healing exactly as I have described it here.

The second way of approaching this can be used instead of, or in conjunction with, the first. It's an age old technique, but it can really help. It's simply this. Sit down with a pen and paper (don't use a keyboard, it's too impersonal), and write your younger self a letter. Tell him or her that you understand how they felt. Explain why you're sorry that they went through what they went through. Tell them that it wasn't their fault. Explain the situation honestly, with the intention of providing explanation from your adult perspective which re-writes negative beliefs which may have been carried since then. Promise to look after them from now on. Then, of course, speak anything you think you would like to say to them. This may be quite an emotional process, but it can be hugely cathartic, and it will have the effect of galvanising the facts in your own mind in a way which will be extremely supportive. Keep the letter somewhere private, and refer to it on difficult days. It can be re-written or updated at any time, particularly if you have new insights and understandings which appear through the passage of time. Remember that it is in the **doing** of this that you will receive the benefits. It's not enough to know that you could do it, or just imagining it. You need to actually write the words on the page.

Nobody Can Insult You Without Your Permission

With practice, the above exercises will help you to have a much greater sense that you are on your own team. Though the exercises are simple, the message that they send back to your deeper self is that you've got your own back. This translates into a genuine sense of liking yourself. I mean why would you bother to sit with yourself profoundly if you didn't like yourself? I hope this makes sense? It's lovely to say the mantra "I like myself", but it's far more profound to actually take the time to demonstrate that as a true fact with a daily practice. Actions speak louder than words after all. This brings us nicely to the next point.

"Nobody can insult you without your permission."

You may already be familiar with this idea, but even if you've heard it before, please take another look at it. The children's rhyme, "I'm made of rubber, and you're made of glue. Everything you say to me, bounces off and sticks to you" means what it says. Think of something that you know you are pretty good at. Now imagine that I'm there telling you I think you're rubbish at that thing. Are you hurt? Does it make you feel angry? The very fragile may say yes, but most of us will say something like "Whatever! I've been doing that for twenty years. I don't need to prove myself". The insult is water off a ducks back. The mud doesn't stick. This is what is meant. The insult only affects you if you also "endorse" it as if it were true.

If you think about it carefully, you'll recognise that this ability to rebuff insults is a powerful antidote to anger. Anger is all about feeling attacked in some way. If those attacks slide off you like egg on a new Teflon pan, you won't worry about them, and you won't react. Insults will become meaningless to you. They just won't stick! That's why we're doing the self-protection, self-love exercises. The funny thing is we are our own harshest judges. We internalise the voice of all the critics in our history and then mistake it for our own. But what if those voices had been supportive, and loving? Would we still feel like there's something wrong with us? Of course not! It's all lies in the end anyway. By recognising that all of the insults we've ever received are simply the wounded-ness of other people who are trying to make themselves feel better by making someone else feel worse, we can step into empowerment. We can learn to rebuff their insults, and say "You know what? Good luck with your opinions, you're welcome to them. You can't take anything away from me that I'm not willing to give you. And, one thing I'm not going to give you is the power to hurt me. You may not like me, but I like me. So, no, I disagree with your insult. I AM okay thanks!"

You need to like yourself to be able to do this. Liking yourself, and wanting to improve yourself do not need to be mutually exclusive. It would be easy to fall into the trap of thinking that you can only like yourself if "X" condition is met. The idea here is to recognise that we are all works in progress, and we all deserve to start out with a fundamental feeling of self-worth. As long as you are willing to extend this same respect to other peoples' self-worth, it is a logical place to arrive at. None of us can go very far without a basic sense of self-worth. Stop thinking of it as an unobtainable privilege, and start recognising that it's a human right. If you're hugely judgemental towards others, then now is the time to realise that you won't be nice to yourself unless you can also be nice to others. That's just logic. If you're judgemental, of course you'd expect others to be too. People are probably a lot more judgemental of me than I care to realise. That's fine. I choose to live in a World where I judge others as little as possible, and hope they'll do the same for me. If they don't, I don't consider it my problem. It's theirs. They'll get what they expect, and I'll get what I expect.

You can like yourself and still recognise that you are working to improve yourself. You just need to set the bar a bit lower to begin with, meaning that liking yourself as you are starts with being a bit more forgiving of yourself for your faults. Human beings are not perfect. You can like yourself because you're doing your best with what you have, and where you are right now. If others wish to stand in judgement of you, that's up to them. It doesn't mean you have to agree with them!

CONSTRUCTIVE CRITICISM

With this understood, we need to be able to handle **some** criticism. A failure to listen to constructive criticism is a big trigger for angry people. You lose in two ways. First of all everyone who loves you is too afraid to offer you meaningful advice. They know you'll take it badly, so they remain silent. The outcome is that you miss valuable opportunities to learn. The second loss is the constant stress of feeling like you're being attacked by the World at large and you may miss larger opportunities as a result.

It's difficult to accept criticism. Our egos are very protective, and the less self-worth you have generally, the more powerful that response is likely to be. It is a hugely liberating step however to make a conscious decision to stop listening to those knee-jerk angry reactions to anything which you perceive as an attack upon your worth or opinion and take a step back for a moment. Instead of immediately assuming that somebody is intending to attack you, ask a question first.

Might there actually be a helpful message for me here?

I want to share a quick story with you which will illustrate this point. Back in 1992, I was an angry young man. I had reason to be. My life circumstances were extremely stressful. There was a difficult economic recession taking place at that time, and I was an unskilled worker. I fell in love with an American girl and we were trying to be together. She already been deported once because we didn't meet the immigration requirements, and I was fighting to get her resident status here in the UK. There was a huge amount of uncertainty, and my job only paid junior wages. I was commuting into Central London and working for a bank in the City as a temp. One day, I had a bit of a run-in with my immediate manager. I angrily ranted at her about what a pile of crap I thought the job was, and how unfairly I thought we (I had a co-worker) were being treated, and what a bunch of stuck up people worked here. Some of my points were valid, but launching an attack like that at her was out of order. I had an attitude and she knew it. I risked being fired. She gave me a good talking to. She was actually a lovely lady, but I was so angry that I couldn't see it. She didn't talk down to me. She said something along the lines of "Look John...these are tough times. Everyone is living on the edge right now. None of us know how secure our jobs are. We all just need to be grateful for what we have". My internal response was "Pah! What a load of crap!" I didn't feel listened to. I felt dismissed, and I resolved to remain in my funk. About a week later, I was doing some self-development meditation, and in the coolness of a different space I had a profound experience. I saw that conversation replayed in my mind's eye, only this time, I saw it from the perspective of a fly on the wall. As I watched the replay, I suddenly had this deep sense that the universe was speaking to me through her. I know how hokey this sounds, but it was truly liberating. I listened to her message again, and now it sounded really benevolent.

76

Now the subtext changed. Instead of hearing "You're being an ar*****e, don't be so f*****g ungrateful", I heard "I know you're in pain John. I like you. I don't want you to feel so wound up all the time. Try to calm down and get through this difficult time with as little stress as possible. I am on your side, but my hands are tied right now". When I returned to work on Monday, I resolved that I should make every effort to be less angry, and I apologised to her for my recent behaviour. She was really sweet about it. I felt better, and my change of attitude was noted. Soon afterwards she really stuck up for us with senior management and we were made permanent members of staff with a pay rise and full staff benefits. I have no doubt that this was as a result of me changing my attitude.

Accepting that you might be in the wrong or considering whether criticism might be constructive is challenging. It doesn't come easily to anybody, so think of it as a life skill. It's something you can learn to do with practice, and it's something you will need to **choose** to do. When you master it, you will find that life is actually a richer place as you listen to the messages that people bring you. They can be very valuable. I hope this story illustrates that you can often gain something by making that choice. Again, we see that softness controls hardness.

IT ALL DEPENDS ON HOW YOU LOOK AT IT

If you've been reading the book without practicing the exercises, it will at this point be an intellectual journey only. That's absolutely fine. I hope it's helped anyway. You can of course read the book to get the whole picture and then come back and do the exercises when you're ready. All I will say is that it's only by actually engaging with the exercises that you will receive the full benefits of the understanding presented. Do be sure to return to Chapter Five at the end of the book to work with the relevant exercises.

If you **have** been practicing the exercises of regular relaxation and meeting your wounded feelings with empathy, understanding, and reassurance, then I hope you're noticing a difference! If your practices have been successful so far, you should be experiencing a decrease in stress levels and finding it much easier to approach stressful situations without those powerful automatic reactions triggering so easily. If that's you, well done!

The exercises so far have been designed to help resolve those triggers which are caused by faulty templates in the **subconscious** limbic system library. Both the reduction of stress generally, and the re-writing of old belief systems should help enormously. So, if you've been doing the exercises, you should now be in a position where you are no longer dominated by overpowering gut reactions to perceived slights against you. This paves the way for you to now be able to **consciously** work with your angry patterns without being overwhelmed in the process. In short, you should now be in control to a level where the tools I am about to give you will actually work. If you've tried anger management tools before and found them ineffective, it's probably because your subconscious mind was holding on to a protective agenda which no amount of willpower could override. Assuming that you are no longer carrying a deeply wounded sense of self, you'll now find that your efforts to make changes won't be thwarted at every turn. In fact, you will be pleasantly surprised by just how easily change can now come. There's still work to do though.

At one level, anger is also a habit, and an addiction, and like any habit or addiction, it will present itself to you as a friend. It will woo you with its promise of power and control, and then it will ruin your life the moment your back is turned. Uncontrolled anger is not your friend. We need to ensure that we don't hold a welcome door open for it. So the first thing I ask you to do is to be clear in your own mind that uncontrolled anger can no longer be welcomed in your life. You need to make a sincere commitment to recognising that anger itself is the enemy. Do be clear that this not an invitation to berate oneself for having angry feelings once in a while. As we've discussed, that is human, and actually we want to learn to channel anger appropriately and make an ally of it. When I say anger can no longer be welcomed, I'm saying that a commitment is required to stop **being** angry as a lifestyle.

There are at least thirty moments in anybody's day which could potentially create an angry response. It's not that other people don't have those moments too. It's simply that they meet them without too much resistance. The first thing to recognise is that life is filled with potential irritations. The goal here is to become an expert in, to borrow someone else's phrase, "not sweating the small stuff". If your anger is triggered thirty times a day over minute details, you're doing it out of habit. That's not because you have a major unresolved anger issue. That's because at some level, it gives you something, just like an addiction. But, trust me. It's taking more than it gives! I know the distinction is subtle, but please recognise that there is a difference between feeling anger and being angry.

With that commitment firmly in place we can now turn our attention to the practical matters of reducing the amount of unnecessary anger which is triggered in your life on a daily basis. Before you can fix a habit, you have to make it conscious. You may not even notice how many times a day you "do" anger. It's just a lifestyle. So, the first thing I want you to do is spend the next three days with a piece of paper and a pencil handy. Every time you respond with anger to something, I want you to note it down with a tally mark. Count them up at the end of each day. What have you learned?

So let's take some examples of things which irritated you:-

* *The kids ate all your favourite breakfast cereal.*

* *You couldn't find your wallet before leaving the house*

* *Someone pushed in front of you at the bus queue.*

* *You lost a sales lead at work.*

* *You missed your bus home because a phone call held you up for ten minutes.*

* *You can't concentrate on the TV because there's a dog barking down the street.*

This is all understandably irritating stuff. What needs to be understood though is that anger makes more anger. Everything you respond to with **welcomed** anger will simply make more anger. Let's look at the list with new eyes. Suppose you didn't respond with anger to any of these situations? How could you not? Please don't get me wrong here. What follows is going to seem insultingly simple, and there's every chance that you do make perceptive adjustments like this every day. I don't wish to insult your intelligence, or suggest that chronic anger is all down to being lazy in thinking. That's not my message. I'm using this list simply to illustrate a point which is formulaic. Your buttons will be pushed by different and perhaps more serious things. The point is to understand that you do have optional ways of perceiving.

Here are some suggested alternatives to habitual anger: -

* *The kids ate all your favourite breakfast cereal.*

Your interpretation: - FFS. All I want to do is eat and go. This is f*****g typical in this house! (Kids are resented for eating the cereal and spouse is considered useless for not keeping the cupboards properly stocked).

How you could look at it: - It's no big deal. I'll have some oats. It will only take four minutes in the microwave. I'll go and get my stuff together while it's cooking.

* *You couldn't find your wallet before leaving the house*

Your interpretation: - Goddammit! Why can't I **ever** find anything in this house? It's **always** such a mess (massive resentment towards the kids for the mess they make).

How you could look at it: - Okay. Think for a moment. It has to be somewhere. Where was I last night? Ah...that's right. I popped into the shops on my way home and it's probably in my rucksack (finds wallet there).

* *Someone pushed in front of you at the bus queue.*

Your interpretation: - (Repressing rage) Who do they think they are?! What? Am I invisible?!

80

How you could look at it: - It really doesn't matter who gets on the bus first. It's not going anywhere until we're all on it anyway.

* You lost a sales lead at work.

Your interpretation: - That b*****d promised me he was going to take our product. What a dick!

How you could look at it: - This is business. Some you win, some you lose. I can understand that he had to take the better offer. We have to do the same sometimes.

* You missed your early bus home from work because a phone call held you up for ten minutes.

Your interpretation: - I f*****g hate this place. Now I'll get home to a cold dinner.

How you could look at it: - It's not every day. I'll just phone my partner and let them know I'll be home a bit later. It happens. It's not the end of the World.

* You can't concentrate on the TV because there's a dog barking down the street.

Your interpretation: - I would like to shoot that damn dog! All I want when I get home is a bit of peace and quiet, and I can't even get that! It's not much to ask is it?! (Seethes)

How you could look at it: - Hopefully, it's just a temporary problem. It's probably driving everyone a bit crazy. If it goes on past today, maybe I could ask a few of the neighbours what they think, and we could get something done to get the owner to control the dog better or keep it inside. I'll suck it up for now. (Dog problem resolves itself).

I know that life is rarely this tidy, and as I said, no insult to your intelligence is intended here, but if you are angry thirty times a day, then something **like** this is going on. It's your job to identify those moments and find a different way of interpreting the incoming data which

81

challenges the continuation of anger as a **habitual** response to life. You're going to need to figure it out because it's all these mini-arousals which are pumping up the pressure cooker, and it's only a matter of time then before there's an almighty explosion. Like I said, it is better just not to go there in the first place. Hopefully now you understand what I mean by that?

Quitting this kind of anger is very similar to quitting any other bad habit. It begins with the decision to change the pattern, and from thereon in, it's a case of believing that you can do it, and then doing it. As with all habit breaking, it's largely a matter of doing something differently for long enough that the new pattern becomes established. Think of a huge boulder at the top of a grassy hill. When you push the boulder over the edge, it rolls to the bottom, and it leaves a groove in the hill. You take the boulder to the top of the hill again, and from the same starting position you repeat over and over. Eventually the boulder wears a large channel into the hillside. This is how habit operates within the brain. Instead of grassy hills, we wear channels of behaviour into our neural pathways which soon make the habit automatic. In order to create a new channel, you have to start the boulder out from a different place on the hill. At first the groove will be shallow and the boulder might keep rolling out as it hits a stone, but with repetition, eventually the boulder will make a deep enough groove that it stays in the channel. Building new habitual responses is the same principle. You have to keep lifting the boulder into its new channel until the channel is deep enough to keep the boulder on course automatically. Then it becomes the new "normal" for you, and you won't have to work at it any more.

Is this profound advice? Not really. But an interesting fact of psychology is that people are more likely to do something if they understand WHY it's worth doing. What I hope to have established for you so far is the understanding necessary to know why breaking this habit is worth doing, and a little bit of faith that the work you do will yield positive results. Now we have the why, let's move on to the how.

CHAPTER SIX – NEW PERSPECTIVES

So, let's begin with the habit. You understand the principle, but you're still not sure how to actually put it into practice. The first thing is to reduce your stress levels generally. The anger management relaxation recording I've included for download with this book will help you to do that. In addition to this the download includes very specific hypnotic suggestions designed to help you break the habit of reacting angrily. You will note that the recording repeats the suggestion that you can learn to **respond** instead of **react.** This is important to understand. **Reaction** is reactive. It's knee-jerk, instinctive, possibly violent, and uncontrolled. It's what your limbic system does when it senses a threat. **Response** is considered, and controlled. So, the goal is to learn to respond rather than react. That involves taking a mental step back from the situation in order to move your brain into a different place. There are various ways to do this. Again, this is not particularly profound advice, and you've doubtless heard it before, but there's a reason it's enduring advice. Put simply, it does the job. Here it is...drum roll...cymbal crash. **Count to fifteen before you do anything.** That's it. Make a contract with yourself to count to fifteen, slowly, every time you feel an angry response coming on. And breathe! Take some conscious breaths with the intention of calming your brain. If you've been using the relaxation recording you're going to find this much easier because those hypnotic suggestions will have conditioned your mind to the feelings of relaxation you experience when using the recording. These are called post-hypnotic suggestions, meaning that they become active after the session, when the required anchor point happens. In the recording, the anchor point is "Should you ever feel anger rising...." The recording doesn't include the suggestion to count, but that doesn't matter. It **does** include the suggestion that you will be able to respond rather than react, and counting is responding. If you're not using the recording, you can still count and breathe. It's going to make a difference. If fifteen seconds doesn't do it, then make it thirty. Give yourself time to cool down, and have the **intention** to cool down. Remember, we're talking about breaking a habit here, and we covered earlier the matter of feeling entitled to our anger, and subconsciously wanting to stay angry. You're not going to succeed unless you have the genuine intention to quit anger as a habit. This is going to take work, so you will need to meet those feelings with courage, and be determined not to keep "doing" those old patterns. There is no magic bullet. You just have to want it, and then make it happen. This one is on you. You can do it. You just have to make it your priority. Remember, it will get easier every day that you do it.

While these habits of anger are at one level just a habit and a compulsion, they are also a result of broken rules. Let's see a couple of points from the list again.

Anger causing event*: The kids ate all your favourite breakfast cereal.*

Rules broken: The house should always be fully stocked. The kids should be more thoughtful. My partner should be more thoughtful and tell the kids to save some cereal for me.

What's wrong with these statements? Why are they bound to create anger? Well, the short answer is that they are stuffed full of "should" and in this case, those "shoulds" contain unrealistic expectations. The bar is set way too high. It's just not going to happen in a real live busy house running on a tight schedule. The house is not going to be unfailingly well stocked. Groceries will run out sometimes. The partner is busy too, and doesn't have time to scrutinise the children sat at the breakfast table on their cereal use, and as for the kids being considerate? Er...no! With this being the case, we have to ask who is responsible for this person's anger. Is it the responsibility of the children or the spouse to change the circumstances to meet this person's expectations? Let's assume that they attempt to do so. What would be the result? I imagine that breakfast would then look like a Victorian tea party. The children would be politely and silently sat at the table in prim dress. The partner would be faithfully serving tea from a silver pot. While it may be possible, it won't be relaxed. You'll simply have a tense family. The most logical answer is that this person will need to deal with his or her expectations to bring them into line with reality, rather than try to make reality fit the expectation. That's the path of least resistance. What does that mean in practice? It means "change your rules". If you don't want your rules to be constantly broken, then you have to lower your expectations. You are not the problem. Your children are not the problem. Your partner is not the problem. Your rules are the problem. So let's explore this more fully.

Rules re-written: It would be really nice if the cupboards were always fully stocked, but I know we all lead busy lives and **sometimes** (replaces always) **we'll** ("we" is assuming equal responsibility and ceasing blame) miss something. The kids are thoughtful in their own way. Like when they bring me a picture. Kids aren't aware of consideration in the same way that adults are. It's unreasonable to expect them to be. **I'd love it if** we all had time to keep everything tightly monitored and organised, but these things are part of everyday life. It's unfair to blame anyone. My partner IS thoughtful in so many ways. It's just cereal. I can choose to notice what he or she does do for me instead. Here is another one:-

Anger causing event: You missed your early bus home from work because a phone call held you up for ten minutes.

Rules broken: Customers shouldn't call at 4.59pm when they know we close at 5! Work should always be pleasant (relating to "I hate this place"). I shouldn't have to work beyond my contracted hours. I must catch the early bus home.

Again, we see the words must, should, and always in evidence here. There are expectations being broken, and it creates anger. So, if we don't want anger to dominate, we're going to need to change our rules; that is, lower our expectations. Basically, we need to replace these urgent and inflexible expectations with relaxed flexible ones. That means replacing words like must, have-to, should, shouldn't, can't, never, and always, with words like I'd like to, prefer, could, might, sometimes, and maybe. Notice the difference in how stressful the inflexible words feel compared to the flexible ones. So, here are some re-writes on those stressful rules so that they are much less likely to cause emotional disturbance.

Rules re-written: It would be great if customers didn't call at 4.59 but that's the busy World these days. I can't say I haven't done it myself! **I'd prefer work to be** a joyful place all the time, but the reality is that work is work. I get paid for it. It's okay most of the time. **I'd love it if** I could guarantee that I'd be home by 5.30 every night, but that's really a privilege, not a right. I can give a little bit more when it's needed and feel okay about that. The world won't end if I'm home by six.

I don't want to labour the point, so we'll leave it there. In summary, the principle is that you need to identify which rules are being broken when you feel anger rising, and then **actively** seek out the imperative wording and change it so that it's soft rather than hard. Again, softness controls hardness.

LOOKING FOR THE BEST

When I was about eighteen years old I was a man full of hope. I saw the problems in the World, and I sincerely believed that the World could heal. I knew it was possible, but I was wise enough to know, even then, that it wouldn't happen easily. I remember seeing very clearly the possibility of becoming cynical and jaded, and I made a contract with myself, a promise, to do all that I could do to make sure I never went that way. I'm now almost forty five years old, and it remains an ongoing challenge to maintain a bright and positive outlook. The reality is that the world is terribly corrupt. Corporate interests are placed before humanity's needs. The environment is ravaged by industry. There are religious wars everywhere you look. There is enormous pressure on each of us as individuals to make ends meet. Our cities are more crowded. Our services are overwhelmed, and we live in a system which is increasingly competitive in every respect. These are the hard cold facts of life in the UK in 2016. It's pretty depressing stuff. It's hardly surprising then that we can individually conclude that we now live in a dog-eat-dog world where only the fittest and most ruthless will survive. To my mind, and you're welcome to disagree, this attitude is selling out our humanity. I don't know about you, but that's not the World I want to live in, and I fear that if we individually walk down this path, then collectively there may be no way back. We will become an increasingly selfish, greedy, hostile species which will eventually self-implode. A system based on all taking and no giving ends up with one man with everything and everyone else with nothing. I don't call that wealth.

It is true that we cannot individually change the system in its entirety. The truth is, nobody is in control of this crazy thing we call the World. Where we're heading is anyone's guess. But, the World is comprised of individuals and you do get a single vote. You vote with your being. If you view the World as hostile and ruthless, then that's what it will be. You will go on to edit out kindness and take ruthless action which will only encourage others to do the same as competition forces survival. This is why the World is as it is at this present moment. A minority of people decided that it is better to take than co-operate. It's much easier to destroy something than it is to build something. This minority have acted foolishly. While patting themselves on the back for how clever they are to have fed on all these helpless weak sheep, they have failed to recognise the greater significance of the sheep's efforts. They have confused kindness and co-operation for weakness.

I can't tell you how to think. You'll do what you want to do, I know that, but here's my contention to you. If you look for the worst in the World that's not only what you'll find, but also what you'll get. You'll also do damage along the way. Ruthless action will undo the hard work of the many. This movement of ruthlessness is a tide. It can reach a high point and turn, but that will only happen if we each as individuals decide that a ruthless unkind World is not the one we want for ourselves, or our children. This will ultimately be decided by the actions we take as individuals.

I'm sure that most people reading this don't want this either? You may remember that I said earlier that people need a "why" in order to agree to doing something? Well that's my case. That's the "why", and here's the "how".

So goes the famous old quote "Fool me once, shame on you. Fool me twice, shame on me." I had to deal with this regularly as a therapist. My consulting rooms cost me in the region of ten pounds an hour to rent. If somebody didn't arrive for their appointment I would lose out in three respects; once because I had to pay for an empty room, twice because I had refused other business, and thrice because I now had no wages for that hour. I soon learned that some people were unreliable. If somebody didn't arrive for their appointment as booked, I would ask for a non-refundable deposit to re-book which would then be held against future late cancellations until the end of their treatment. I knew that if somebody was willing to pay this, then they were serious about their treatment. If they didn't, then it was pretty much guaranteed that they would have fooled me twice, so I wouldn't re-book them. Problem solved.

It's understandable that any of us are forced to protect ourselves in a complex World. I'm not advocating foolhardy good-heartedness which leaves us open to loss and attack. I'm simply suggesting that everybody deserves a chance to show that their intentions are good before we decide that they are not. It is true that we will experience some losses by taking this approach, but if you look at it through a business lens, every business has to account for bad debts at the end of the accounting year. It goes with the territory of extending credit. Business can't operate without credit and neither can we. Our credit is our goodwill.

So here's the rule. Give everybody a chance to show you they can do the right thing. Obviously don't be reckless with this. If a guy phones you up and tells you you've won a million pounds but first he needs your credit card details to process the funds, then that's not the right time to extend trust. Clearly, this is one of the wolves. Putting aside situations where you could be genuinely burned however, it really pays to expect the best from people. It's another interesting fact of psychology that people tend to like people who they can help. There's a feel good factor in helping people. In other words, most people **want** to extend positive intention towards you. They get something from treating you well which costs you nothing. If you know that people around you aren't of this nature, then you're probably hanging out with the wrong crowd. Get some new friends. Most people are generally good-hearted souls trying to get on in the World and enjoy each other's company. Most people don't want to harm you or rip you off. In short, look for the best in people, and don't let anyone fool you twice. If you're willing to risk being fooled once, you'll find that it's a fantastic investment. Sure, you will make some losses along the way, but you'll gain far more than you venture, and you'll end up with a pool of reliable people in your life who want to help you. This is a self-fulfilling prophecy which will take you, and perhaps just as importantly, us, in a direction we want to go. An adversarial outlook will lead to a mean World. Co-operation will lead to abundance. It's a good World with some bad stuff in it. Make sure you're a builder, and remember that kindness isn't a weakness; it's strength.

DEALING WITH CONTROLLING BEHAVIOUR

This is potentially a serious matter. First of all, if you are angry because you are in a situation in which someone is exhibiting controlling behaviour towards you, then you really need to do everything within your power to leave that situation as soon as is humanly possible. No good can come of remaining in this type of situation. Although it is possible for people to change, the likelihood is that they won't, even if they say that they will, unless they demonstrate some serious action to get professional help. As I hope I've illustrated, no amount of goodwill can last without a deeper resolution of the reasons for their anger, defensiveness, and paranoia. They will continue to attack. Insist that they get help, or leave. If you fear for your life, or your safety, there are organisations out there which can help and give you refuge. These situations can escalate to murder. I know it is complex, and will probably challenge you to your core, but having some support will make things much clearer. Pick up the phone and do it today. Sorry for the stark warning, but that's the way it is.

If you are the one doing the controlling behaviour, then take note. This is serious. If you're not already at the place where you are a danger to yourself or others, then be aware that you **may** be heading that way if you don't resolve this problem. If you've already done harm, please, please get professional help. I'm sure you really don't want that. As I mentioned earlier this can be a form of Obsessive Compulsive Disorder, and whatever the case you may need more than this book to resolve the difficulty. There are many organisations and charities which can offer you immediate support. This is an illness, and you need to recognise it as such. Please also pick up the phone, and speak to someone. You will be surprised to find that it's not such an unsympathetic World after all. There are people out

89

there who won't judge you, and will **want** to help. Stop kidding yourself that you can handle it all on your own. Be courageous. It will be the best thing you've ever done.

With that serious note now noted, let's take things down a notch. Many forms of controlling behaviour aren't yet this serious, and wouldn't be classed as OCD. That's probably most people reading. Now, there's every chance that if you've successfully implemented the understanding presented so far, you'll be actually moving away from the urge to control everything. As your limbic system arousal reduces, and you shift your perspectives towards softness and healing, you'll feel much less threatened, which will translate as less need to control everything. Still, like any habit, you may find those behaviours still in evidence so let's understand how you can make things better.

We need to understand how the limbic system operates in this regard. Every time you carry out a controlling behaviour, you inadvertently send a message back to the clunky old limbic system that you "agree" with the assumption that the behaviour is necessary. The limbic system receives that message as confirmation that it is promoting a helpful strategy for you to have your needs met, and your safety secured. It then decides that "do more of that in future" is the correct course of action, and duly obliges by sending you more fear, and stronger signals to control everything. This is why controlling behaviour can escalate to catastrophic levels. The sufferer can experience increasing anxiety when they don't do the behaviour. When it's a toss-up between feeling really anxious or doing a controlling behaviour, the controlling behaviour appears to be the path of least resistance. Thus, a negative cycle strengthens. This is an insatiable beast. The feelings will say "Just do it one more time and then everything will be okay". That's a lie. It won't. It will only make more of the feelings, and drive you to do more of the behaviours. So, how do we end this cycle?

You need to recognise that the feeling that you need to control a situation is in fact an **erroneous** message originating in the feeling brain. It is not a fact. It is just a feeling which drives you to "do" that behaviour, and it is fundamentally a lie. We've already established that anger makes more anger. We know that softness controls hardness. We know that anger ruins lives. We know that anger is often a cover for hurt and anxiety. We know that by trying to control everything we get the exact opposite of what we want because we drive everything we love away. So, you tell me. How exactly is controlling behaviour going to help you? It just won't work. So, when you look at it with this clarity, there's no discussion to be had. The feeling that controlling behaviour will help you to get what you want is a lie. It won't. It will give you the opposite. Therefore, the **feeling** is in error. Now, with that firmly established, the next step is to refuse to do the behaviour. That means, no matter how anxious it makes you to not do it, you still must not do it!

So, you're feeling like your partner might be cheating on you. You start checking his/her phone while they're out. You find nothing, but you carry on checking. What message are you sending to your limbic system? You're convinced that your business partner is taking money out of the business. You have checked the accounts fifty times already and there's no evidence of any bad dealings, but you still check every day. What message are you sending to your limbic system? You're sure your best friend is deliberately avoiding you. You send them a friendly text. They don't reply. You obsessively check your phone every five minutes for a week, becoming progressively angrier every time there's no reply. What message are you sending to your limbic system? Then the controlling behaviours begin. You decide to start calling your partner through the day to say Hi, except you're not just saying Hi. You're listening intently for any evidence of someone else being with them, or any sign that they might not be where they said they'd be. You start asking probing questions of your business partner. They sense your mistrust and start to distance themselves. This convinces you that they are hiding something. You start bombarding your friend with passive-aggressive texts. Actually, they were just busy and meant to get back to you and it slipped their mind, but now they're freaked out by your texts and **actually** don't want to get back to you! Do you see where this is going?

There is only one way to stop this, and that is to STOP THIS! Look, no amount of checking is going to stop any negative action. If people are going to hurt you, they are going to hurt you. What other people do is not within your control. At best, you can influence the situation by making sure that you're not the one giving someone reason to like you less, and act negatively towards you. We're back to giving everyone ONE chance to

91

show you that their intentions are positive towards you. This is just what life is. There is uncertainty. Relationship is risk. We need to **presume innocence** unless proven otherwise. Stick to the one chance rule, and consider all other forms of paranoia to be exactly that. Unless you have evidence that people are treating you badly, begin with the assumption that they are not. That means that the feeling that something is wrong **is an anxiety**, not a truth, and certainly not a betrayal. Treat it as such. It's not about them, it's about you. You have to resist the urge to do the checking behaviour. If you do this for long enough, eventually it will fade, in exactly the same way that someone who quits smoking will eventually find that the urge to smoke will fade.

What you are effectively doing is saying to the limbic system "I'm afraid you have it wrong." You then **refuse to carry out the controlling behaviour**, and you act **as if** nothing is wrong. You **will** still have those feelings, but if you are consistent with your refusal to act irrationally upon them, your limbic system will eventually make the necessary adjustment, and they'll fade in time. It's not easy at first, but it is how you escape the cycle of controlling behaviour, and you must know that it will get easier in time. Be determined. This is your life you are working to heal. You cannot afford to not deal with this. Your efforts will be rewarded. If you need further help with this, it really might be worth seeking the help of a therapist. Most will be experienced in dealing with these matters, and you could be surprised by how far a little bit of help can go. It's worth considering.

Chapter Seven – Anger In Relationships

Anger is the instinctive mechanism by which nature protects itself against violation. Here's the dictionary definition of violation: -

* *To break or fail to comply with a rule or formal agreement.*

* *Failure to respect someone's peace, privacy, or rights.*

* *To invade, trespass upon, encroach upon, or intrude upon.*

* *To treat something sacred with irreverence or disrespect.*

* *To assault someone.*

These definitions encompass pretty much everything which can cause a person to become angry. We've already shown how much of our anger is triggered unnecessarily because our rules are too rigid, or we are seeing threat where none is intended as a result of muddy filters, wounded-ness or fear. Sometimes however, anger is entirely appropriate, and entirely justified. When that is the case, anger can become a powerful ally, and we need to learn to channel that anger with Kung Fu focus and make it work for us, rather than against us. Uncontrolled anger will usually bring about a worsening of the situation. If we can channel the anger in a controlled way, it can become true power. This involves a cool head and a steady heart.

Let's look at how we could channel anger appropriately to protect ourselves against violation.

If we want people to respect our rules, rights, property, reputation, time, energy, and safety, we need to begin with the question "Are my rules fair and meaningful, and are other people actually **able** to comply with them?" If your rules are unreasonably restrictive, or contravene the rights of others, you should not be surprised if people break them, or are hostile in response. My mother had a rule that things should **never** get lost. As a child, I lived in terror of her losing a hairbrush, or God forbid, that I might lose something which belonged to her. She would go berserk, and there would be a rampage to follow. The fact is things are going to get lost sometimes. It's an unreasonable rule. If your rule isn't in line with reality, change it. Then you won't get angry. End of story.

Assuming that you have a reasonable rule though, the next thing is to make sure that other people know about it! Remember the frying pan incident? That was a case of unsynchronised rulebooks. If that lady had communicated to me that she would like the frying pan washed after each use, I would have explained the situation, apologised for unintentionally disrespecting her space, changed my frying pan habits, and we would have remained friends no doubt.

I learned a valuable lesson in communicating rules early on in my career as a therapist. There I was at the end of a tough training regime. Mountains had been moved, and I was in my first few weeks of business. Although I later changed the model I used altogether, I was initially trained to offer a free one hour initial consultation to prospective clients. I had paid for my consulting rooms, and I had a five hour slot with four new clients booked in for that afternoon. The CD's were ready, the paperwork was all nicely presented, and I was excited to get the show on the road. I eagerly awaited the buzzer at 1.30pm. At 1.40pm, there was still no sign of my client. At 1.45pm, I called their mobile. It was switched off. I'd been let down. Oh well. Onwards and upwards I thought. I looked at four walls for forty five minutes and at 2.30pm I eagerly awaited my next client. At 2.40pm there was no sign of him. This continued for the rest of the day. I had busted my back to get to this moment, and not one of the four arrived! I spent almost five hours sitting in an empty room which had cost me sixty pounds to hire, twiddling my thumbs, with nothing but disappointment and a sense of stranger betrayal to keep me company. I was genuinely heartbroken. I was also pretty darn irritated.

At the time, I was finishing my work with my own therapist, and at our next session I recounted the experience and shared my absolute despondency at the situation. She said "Do you have a cancellation policy?" "Er....No.....I don't", I replied. "And the first session is free?" she asked. "That's right" I said. "So, what are you doing then to communicate to people that your time is valuable and not to be wasted? How can you expect people to respect your energy and time if you tell them it's free and there are no consequences to not arriving? You're basically communicating that it's a commitment-free arrangement with no value. Of course they'll let you down. You've invited them to do so." Well, of course that's not how I'd been thinking about it. In my book of rules it's a given that when you make an appointment, you keep it. My mistake was assuming that just because that was obvious to me, I was assuming that everyone else works to the same rules. Evidently, they don't! So, the first lesson here is this. If you want people to work to your rules, then it's your responsibility to make sure that the rules, your expectations, are spelled out clearly, and I mean with crystal clarity. They can't be vague or hopeful. They need to be explicit and definite. I **used** that anger to take appropriate action. Here's what I did. I implemented a cancellation policy. I explained that a failure to attend a "free" initial consultation would mean that the full fee would be payable, in advance, if they failed to attend without due notice, and wished to re-book. I also wrote a welcome document which went with each written appointment confirmation to every client booking covering exactly what our respective responsibilities were to the therapeutic relationship. Here's the wording I used for the relevant section: -

Your Courtesy (i) – Apart from the obvious courtesy two people naturally extend to each other, here I am specifically referring to your booked appointments. If for any reason you can't make an appointment, please let me know as far in advance as possible if you think you won't be able to make it. I may then be able to re-use the appointment slot, or at the very least I may be able to schedule the rest of the day productively. If there are genuine reasons you can't make an appointment, then just call. I'll be happy to re-book you (subject to cancellation policy). I'm not an ogre. If you're unwell or have a genuine emergency I obviously won't ask for a missed appointment fee, but please do me the courtesy of letting me know if you can't make it. You can call either myself directly on ********* (leave a message if I'm not there) or the Therapy Centre on **********.

This may appear to be slightly uptight, but I can tell you that it did the job it was intended to do. The shift in client respect towards my time went from one to nine and a half overnight. I later stopped offering free one hour initial consultations at the consulting rooms too. I found that a free hour of consulting time was a waste of therapy time and still encouraged the uncommitted through my door, so I switched to a free telephone consultation followed by a longer first working session. I still offered a free hour, but I changed the format so as to screen potential clients, and only invited the most committed people to work with me. If they weren't committed at the telephone consultation stage, I wouldn't invite them in. My practice was often over-subscribed so I had the luxury of only inviting in people who really were willing. Again, it was a hugely successful change, and my practice was altogether better for it. I'm quite sure it benefitted my clients equally, as with the question marks dealt with, they arrived committed, and that meant we could get to work straight away. Here's the wording I used for my cancellation policy: -

Missed Appointments

Consulting hours are limited and pre-booked. The costs involved in hiring professional consulting rooms are substantial, and I pay for room hire regardless of whether the room is used or not. So, whilst I do recognise that the majority of clients are most conscientious, I ask for your understanding in having to advise that missed appointments will need to be paid for to cover room costs and a proportion of loss of earnings. Therefore, please note:-

I reserve the right to charge a late cancellation fee of £30 for appointments missed or cancelled with less than 48 hours notice. I really don't want to ask for missed appointment fees. I would much rather see you than ask you for money for a missed appointment! Late cancellation fees are easily avoided. Simply let me have at least 48 hours notice and I may be able to offer the appointment slot to someone else.

I still had people mess me about of course, and rarely was the fee collectable. That's just a business loss in any business, but worrying about lost earnings wasn't my primary motivation for the notice. The notice was really a polite and firm way of saying "Don't waste my time", and if you do you'll be paying for it from hereon in.

I channelled my anger in a **controlled** way, to protect myself as far as possible from violation. I never again suffered real anger when someone didn't show up. I just asked them for a deposit and that would sort the committed from the insincere. In short, I didn't get burned twice very often. Occasionally, I'd extend the benefit of the doubt to someone and re-book them without insisting on a deposit. Sometimes they'd still let me down again. They never got another chance. It was my choice to do this though, and I would swallow the loss, with the attitude that I'd rather live in a World where goodwill exists than become so cynical as to never extend trust to anyone again. If someone let me down twice, I mainly just felt sorry for them. I probably could have helped them...if they'd let me.

Have a think then about what rules or agreements are broken in your World, and ask yourself firstly, whether you have actually successfully, and explicitly let the people around you know that they are your rules? There's literally no point in being angry because someone breaks your rules if you haven't told them what the rules are. If your rules are reasonable, the next step is to find an assertive, but **graceful** way to clarify and communicate those rules out into the World. What does that look like for you? Does that mean a sign in your shop window or an announcement on your website? Does it require a letter to a customer to reiterate your terms of business, possibly with penalties for breaching the agreement? Does it mean a team meeting to explain what is considered acceptable behaviour to you as a manager? Does it mean not saying yes to something you want to say no to? Does it mean not letting someone treat you badly? I hope so. Sometimes respect has to be demanded. There are graceful ways to do this. It will be ineffective if your communication is not graceful and diplomatic. Words are truly more powerful than violence in the context of our day to day lives.

ALL YOU NEED TO DO IS ASK

I live in the real world too. Untold atrocities happen in this World every day. It's depressing. Nothing good comes from uncontrolled anger. There are bad people out there who wish to do others harm. If you're in their path, you may need to put your peaceful ways to one side to deal with the situation. Even the Buddhist philosophy, which is probably the most peaceful ideology on the planet, recognises the right to self-defence. When someone is determined to harm you, words may be useless. So let's be clear that this is understood, but, that's not what I'm talking about here.

This is about the everyday experiences you have which leave you feeling angry.

Many people will be reading this book because of the effect that anger is having on their personal and romantic relationships. I've worked with countless people who have told me that they are very controlled when they are at work, but have no patience once they get home. This in itself is quite telling. It tells us that people can exercise control when they have to, but the effort required to keep a lid on it fails when there is "permission" to do otherwise. There is an assumption that our loved ones will forgive an outburst much more readily than a customer or our boss will. In any case, the last thing anyone actually wants to do is misdirect their daily anger at their loved ones, the people who least deserve it. With that said, there may be genuine cause for anger at home too. The same principle is at work here. Which rules are being broken? Are your rules reasonable? Have you communicated your rules clearly to the people you are in relationship with?

Now, we have to recognise that relationships require compromise. Putting it bluntly, no-one is perfect. If I choose to focus in a certain way, I can find something that irritates me about just about everyone I know. I'm also aware that everyone I know can find something about me to be irritated by. Hell, I irritate myself sometimes! I'm sure you do too. If you don't, let me assure you that you are guilty of double standards! So the smart thing to do is just to acknowledge this fact with softness. We are creatures who strive for perfection in an imperfect World. Having a brain can be a pain in the butt. It's prone to judgement, and anxieties, and worries, and depressions, and we are all flawed as a result. We need to recognise this for what it is, and understand that no amount of wishing will change the facts. Then, we can make our peace with the situation quite easily. We simply have to choose to overlook our respective (perceived) flaws with gentleness. You know, my friend Kevin (these are fictional characters by the way) irritates me because he's always late. Beverly gets on my nerves because she's highly opinionated. Fred mumbles his words and doesn't ever say what he means. Jayne gets too drunk when we go out for a meal. Dave repeats himself and tells the same stories over and over. But, I love them. They are my friends. We have fun, and they have many other endearing qualities. I'm willing to overlook their idiosyncrasies. If they make me angry, that's MY problem, not theirs. No amount of me telling Fred to speak properly, Jayne to drink less, or Beverly to get over herself is likely to change them. In fact, a central theme in CBT is that you can't change other people. They are what they are. Choosing to be in relationship with people is accepting the full package, their good bits, and their not so good bits, and loving them anyway. So goes the saying "Be kind – for everyone you meet is fighting a great battle". This is the "why". You'll recognise that this once again means lowering your expectations. If you do that, you're less likely to have your rules broken. Agreed?

With that established, it's no good ignoring an elephant in the room. Real conflicts are going to require proper attention, and cannot simply be overlooked. Although we have said that we have no power to change other people, we can let them know that their behaviours are harmful or unacceptable to us, and ask them to help with a solution to the problem. We can't change them, but if we can explain why we would like them to change their behaviour towards us, that's another matter entirely. This is how we avoid "controlling" behaviour. If you think about it logically, you'll recognise that asking someone to change their behaviour, and attempting to control someone's behaviour, have roughly the same intention and agenda. They both seek to protect you from harm. It's simply that the former might work, and the latter will give you the exact opposite of what you want or need. The reason for this is quite simple. People don't like being "told" what to do! Do you? When someone tells you what to do, what is your first instinct? For most people it's to push back. We take it as an affront to our independence and do the exact opposite in defiance. If someone explains to you however that something you are doing is causing them harm in some way, and **asks** politely whether you may be able to help them find a way to resolve the harmful situation, then you will feel much more inclined to consider the matter thoughtfully, and probably kindly.

Nonviolent Communication

Nonviolent Communication is a model developed by Marshall B. Rosenberg. He says "When we focus on clarifying what is being observed, felt, and needed rather than on diagnosing and judging, we discover the depth of our own compassion. Through its emphasis on deep listening - to ourselves as well as others - NVC fosters respect, attentiveness, and empathy, and engenders a mutual desire to give from the heart."

Some would say that nonviolent communication is too wishy-washy for our fast paced, sometimes cut-throat World. To my mind we have two options. We can fight for survival, or we can co-operate for it. If a solution can be achieved in which everybody gains something, then that is surely preferable? Another complaint against NVC is the notion that it must involve suppression of one's anger. This is hugely inaccurate. It is in fact the very opposite of that. It encourages appropriate expression and communication of one's true feelings. So let's take a look at a fictional situation and explore how it works. This is necessarily simplified for illustration purposes. I recognise that in the real World problems are often much more complex than this, but let's understand the basic principle. Here's the scenario: -

Samantha and Mark have been married four years. Samantha is a stay-at-home mum to two small children. Mark works full time. There are problems in the marriage. Mark thinks that Samantha never stops nagging him, and Samantha says Mark doesn't help out at all with the children. There are frequent rows which end up with Mark telling Samantha that he's sick of her nagging, and Samantha telling Mark he's "f*****g useless!" If this impasse continues, their marriage will be over by Christmas. So what's going on?

Well, both Sam and Mark are equally responsible. They don't see it that way though. They see the other as the problem. The more Sam tells Mark he's a waste of space, the more he resents her and withdraws making him less inclined to help out. The more Mark refuses to help out, the more Sam feels powerless to do anything but try to get her message across. She ends up nagging, and making sarcastic personal comments which deepen the rift. This is a violent and aggressive situation. Each has retreated to their corner, and they are now shouting messages to each other from opposite sides of the globe.

Both are now more focussed on defending their territory rather than looking for a solution. The resentment is at peak level, both are angry as hell, and neither one of them is going to be the one to back down. They've almost forgotten what they are fighting about. All that matters now is the winning.

So, let's freeze frame for a moment. Mark is tired. His job is stressful and he's got his own fair share of problems at work. He's concerned that if he starts looking after the children more, Sam will take advantage of his generosity, and then he'll be lumbered, while she starts kicking back in the evening, and he doesn't see that as fair because he's working too, and putting the money into the home. He looks forwards to coming home at the end of the day, and then when he gets there he wishes he was somewhere else!

Samantha is also tired. She wants some respite from the job of being the full time caregiver for the two little ones. She also wants to feel like an attractive and desired woman. She hasn't worn nice clothes recently because she's been dealing with child vomit on the shoulder for the last year. She's lonely, and feels like a slave in the house.

It is a difficult situation. Are either of them bad people for wanting what they want? I certainly wouldn't say so. It's a common dynamic.

Here are the principles of non-violent communication: -

* **Each is responsible for his own life** – This means that you assume responsibility for your own words, actions, and feelings. Marcus Aurelius said "If you are distressed by anything external, the pain is not due to the thing itself, but to your estimate of it; and this you have the power to revoke at any moment." It's a tough one to agree with, but it remains ultimately true. Remember, nobody can insult you without your permission. If you want to sidestep an insult or attack, you can. Locking horns is not the only option available to you

* **Do not take responsibility for the feelings of others** – The same principle holds true here, in reverse. It is the responsibility of others to own their own feelings, words, and deeds too. If somebody decides to take offence to you when none is intended, that is their cross to bear and resolve, not yours.

* **One cannot force others to feel, think or act the way one wishes** – This we've pretty much covered in detail. Controlling doesn't work.

* **Judging oneself and others often stops honest communication** - By the time you've judged a person as "wrong", you're already planning your attack. A simple fact of psychology is that when people feel attacked they become defensive, but even more importantly here, they stop listening! Think about this for a moment. They literally cannot hear your message

because they are too busy formulating their defence/counter attack. That's how this situation began.

* All people are connected at the level of feelings, basic personality needs, and other levels – This involves being willing to ask yourself what you have in common with the other person. If you were in her/his shoes, wouldn't you also want the same things? This leads to understanding the other person's position, and can help to elicit the necessary empathy for resolution.

In essence NVC is all about stepping out of judgement and reaction, and into careful consideration of the needs of yourself, and others, and looking for a way in which you can work together for an outcome which provides maximum benefit for all parties involved. There is much else in the NVC model which I won't go into here because that's someone else's book. If you'd like to learn more though, the book is still available. It's worth a read.

So, Mark and Samantha need a solution. Potentially there are many solutions to their deepening crisis, and the shape of that solution will depend on many factors, but nothing will be achieved without some clear heart to heart communication. Essentially we're asking "how can they both win?" Ideally, they'll allocate some quality time, free from interruptions, where they can meet in a semi-formal scenario to have the conversation which needs to be had. This example assumes that Mark has taken the initiative to approach a solution. Here's what that successful conversation could look like: -

Mark: I wanted to talk to you about the fact that we've been arguing a lot lately. I'd like to see if we can figure out why, and maybe clear the air a bit?

Samantha: Well, the problem is Mark, that every time I ask you to help out with the Kids you flat refuse and I'm pretty sick of being your house slave! I might as well talk to myself!

Commentary: We are off to a bad start here. Mark has taken the first step, and it probably took a hell of a lot of humble pie to do it too. Samantha is still raising her voice, and still "blaming" Mark. He can't solve this problem alone. He could lose his cool. But no, he's determined that it is time to do something differently. Instead he's going to "yield" to her attack. (Remember, softness controls hardness.)

Mark: (In continued soft voice) I understand that you are angry Sam. I am sorry. I know I haven't been helping you out. I don't think it's good for either of us to stay angry though. I don't want to be angry any more, and you probably don't either, right? So I'm willing to listen to what you have to say, and we can discuss it all properly, and figure out what needs to change. How does that sound?

Samantha: (Softens considerably) Okay. Let's hear it then....

Mark: Okay. Well, it's been pretty stressful in the house right? I've been feeling quite disconnected from you because I feel henpecked sometimes and it doesn't feel much like you want me around in the house. So, I've been thinking. Instead of me just withdrawing, perhaps you can help me to understand what it is that you actually want from me?

Samantha: (Slightly exasperated with raised eyebrows) Really? You don't know? I've only told you like a hundred times!

Commentary: Samantha isn't really helping her own cause here. She's throwing out some hostile comments which could destabilise this important opportunity to create a solution, but she is angry, and Mark continues to allow her to express that without taking it too personally, even though it appears to be directed at him, and it's tough not to shout back. He's looking to connect with the person beyond the pain though, so he perseveres.

Mark: (Still staying cool!) Look, I know you want me to help out with the kids more, but what would that look like, exactly? I guess that you think I should know, but I'd like to be really clear so that I don't unintentionally do the wrong thing.

Samantha: Okay. Well, for starters, it would be a great help if you could bathe Lucy and Will once in a while before bed. I'd just like an hour off sometimes to get my head straight.

Commentary: Mark considers this and feels a surge of anxiety. It's irrational really, but it's automatic. He takes a moment to ask himself why such a feeling could exist, and realises that he feels overwhelmed with the stress from his job, and is reluctant to commit himself to anything which could interfere with his "unwind" time.

Mark: Can I be honest with you Sam? I know it's irrational, but even though I want to help out, I get this really stressed-out feeling when I consider agreeing to that every night. I think I know why. I've been really stressed out at work and it feels like I need every minute I have available just to unwind a bit before it all starts again. I know that's mental, and stupid, but I guess that's why I haven't helped.

Commentary: Samantha isn't sure whether to feel angry or sympathetic. It sounds a bit like a lame excuse, and her first instinct is that Mark needs to man up. They have two kids together! But, she holds back for a moment. She sees he's trying, and makes a conscious decision to take a moment to actually "hear" what he's saying.

Samantha: Well, what's up at work then that's making you feel so stressed out?

Mark: Well, I didn't want to say anything because I didn't want to worry you, but last year they laid off twenty people, and now everyone knows they're looking for the next twenty, so they've upped our targets and I haven't made my target in the last six months. Some of my colleagues are playing dirty, and it's really competitive there now. It's pretty horrible and I don't know what I'll do if they let me go now?

Samantha: Sh*t! You should have told me. I had no idea you had all that going on!

Commentary: Sam's anger starts to melt away. It suddenly becomes clear that Mark's behaviour has been about much more than just being deliberately obstructive.

We could go on, but you can imagine where the rest of this conversation can go now. Mark and Sam continue to dialogue calmly and come to a deeper understanding of their respective stresses. They are now really listening, rather than reacting. They agree that Mark will help out by bathing the kids on Monday, Wednesday, and Friday, and they agree that he'll do some other bits and pieces too. Sam feels truly heard, and suddenly she doesn't feel such a strong sense of overwhelm herself. Mark discovers that bathing the kids three or four times a week helps Sam to de-stress, and he finds that far from being a chore, it's actually a pleasure. The thought of it was much worse than the doing. Sam makes a concerted effort not to nag any more, and agrees that Mark can let her know if he ever feels henpecked and she'll look at it. She starts to make kind little gestures to Mark that make him feel loved. The resentments melt and they start to enjoy each other again, becoming allies rather than enemies. Sam explains her frustration at feeling like a frumpy Mum, so Mark hires a baby sitter and arranges a surprise night out, presenting her with a beautiful new dress to top it off! They schedule in a night out together every fortnight. They talk about the situation at work, and Sam surprises Mark by showing a super supportive side he's never even seen before. He feels relieved to know that he doesn't have to carry that stress all on his own. She tells him that whatever happens, they'll make it work, and she wouldn't think any less of him if his job ends. They agree to keep talking, and listening, and their relationship blossoms again.

This is the **work** everyone talks about in relationships. Some people never make it to this stage. It is work because it involves a continued effort to fight the instinctive urge to react lazily and strike back at any perceived attack. Instead, we need to look beyond the immediate hostility, and invite further communication to investigate together what the true heart of the grievance is. The problem is that we're often arguing about who should do the washing up, when actually we're still sore because of the way our partner spoke to us yesterday. It's not something which will be perfected overnight. It takes repeated effort. Despite Sam and Mark coming to an arrangement here, there will be other disagreements, and they'll need to keep initiating this process. With patience and perseverance, there is every chance of them finding a common ground on all their differences, and learning to treat each other in way which honours those differences.

Two Tangos And A Slice Of Humble Pie

The greatest obstacle to achieving resolution of differences in relationship is our level of willingness to accept that we play a role in the problems in some way. Relationship counsellors will tell you outright that most couples who turn up for counselling are locked into an "I'm right, and you are wrong" struggle. The fact is it takes two to Tango.

Here's a short story which illustrates the point: -

There were two monks walking silently along a riverside. After a while, they happened upon a young lady wearing a beautiful dress, and as they neared, it was apparent that she was in some distress. They stopped and asked what was wrong. The lady explained that there were floods during the week and the bridge had been swept away. She needed to cross the river to get to her sister's wedding. She didn't however want to ruin her dress. The monks were from a sect who forbade physical contact with women, but the elder monk immediately offered to carry the young lady across the river. The younger man was horrified, and admonished his friend explaining that he was breaking his vows and contravening the rules of their religion. The older monk, with the ladies agreement, picked her up, carried her across the river, and put her down on the other side. The Monks continued on their way. The Elder monk received a stream of admonishment from his younger counterpart and listened in silence for some time. Eventually, he turned to his companion and he said "My brother, I put that woman down ages ago. It is you who are still carrying her." One person may have broken the rules, but if you don't let it go, you're continuing the drama.

They say pride comes before a fall, and there are fewer words truly spoken. Admitting we are wrong can feel like a terrible blow to our pride, especially if we've invested a huge amount of energy into protecting our self-importance. Forgiving someone else for the wrong they have done you can equally be perceived as a weakness, but we need to remember what we've learned. Softness controls hardness. Being big enough to let something go is a sign of true strength. There's no rule that says that you have to forgive anyone for anything, but you can be sure that you can't have it both ways. If you can't admit you're wrong, or can't forgive a trespass against you, it's highly unlikely that you'll have a satisfactory relationship with that person again.

Pride can be a very powerful emotion. It's one of the least rational emotions we can experience because pride often chooses to be "right", **whatever the cost**. Sadly, many relationships fail because one or both parties are too proud to admit that they have made mistakes too. Pride has driven people to murder. Consider for instance the obsessive ex who can't get over the fact that their former lover doesn't want to be with them any more. It can be such a blow to pride that it has driven many people to commit unthinkable horrors. It's not to be underestimated. When pride is wounded, it can be tough to get past it, but it's important to understand that the most likely reason a person will find that pride is over-riding logic is because there are unhealed wounds as we discussed in detail at the beginning of the book. Pride, at one level, is a Herculean effort to avoid feeling disempowered. If you can't get past your pride, it's a sure signal that there's something in you which is in need of healing. The wise person will look there, instead of continuing to blame the World. Powerful people don't worry about pride. Here's another illustrative story.

This is called The Gift Of Insults: -

108

An ageing Warrior who had never been beaten in battle accepted the challenge to battle a young, but notoriously fierce Warrior who was passing through the town. His students advised against it because the younger man was infamous for using insults as a means to make his opponents lose their concentration and reveal their weak spots. When the battle commenced, the young man began with his insults, but the experienced ageing Warrior remained in perfect poise. When the insults failed to unsettle his opponent, the younger man turned to spitting, and cussing about his family. Still he remained ready. The young man knew his skills were no match for the lightning hands and fighting experience of the ageing warrior, and after much time he conceded defeat, and walked away in shame.

The students asked their teacher why he didn't teach the insolent youth a good lesson in humility. "Why did you not fight him?" they said. "We know he was no match for your skills. How could you endure such an indignity?"

"If someone brings you a gift, and you choose not to receive it" replied the teacher, "then, to whom does the gift belong?

Nobody can insult you without your permission. Softness controls hardness.

If the situation is that someone else has wronged you, then it's necessary to forgive them if you want to remain in relationship with them. If the situation is that you have wronged somebody and are finding it too much of a blow to your pride to admit it, then you need to learn to forgive yourself. Otherwise you will turn the anger you feel towards yourself for making mistakes into anger towards someone else for unwittingly reminding you of them. This is a deep dynamic, but it is a dangerous one. If you return to the practices in the book, the tools are here to loosen the grip such conflicts may have on your mind. If you need further assistance, see a therapist. They'll help.

We all make mistakes. No one is perfect. It's essential for our mental health that we learn to forgive ourselves for our errors, and essential to the health of our relationships that we learn to forgive others for their errors too. Everyone has moments in their lives they wish they could undo, but we can't. It's done. Ultimately, we have to ask ourselves whether we're more invested in being right and saving face than letting it go. Nobody likes eating humble pie, but coming down from one's high horse is a lot less stress in the long run than remaining right at the cost of everything.

In the end, the solution is to recognise that everyone involved is playing some part in the continuation of the drama. Sometimes you'll never get to the bottom of who was right, and who was wrong. Often, it all depends on how you look at it. The important step is to clarify the rules from hereon in and make the agreement to wipe the slate clean and start again. Don't let pride ruin a good thing. It's a cheap prize for losing everything.

THE POWER OF "SORRY"

The word "sorry" is probably the most powerful word in the English language. If you think about it clearly, you'll recognise that a large proportion of conflicts escalate to anger, rage, and deep resentment precisely **because** the word sorry is not forthcoming. When you're angry, what is it that you really want? Is it possible that the thing you want more than anything is for the person you're angry at to say sorry?

Sorry has the power to save marriages, release people from decades of pain, restore reputations, rekindle friendships, make careers, and resolve wars. A genuine apology communicates so many things. It says "I see your pain. I care about you. I recognise my actions have hurt you. I recognise that your experience is valid. I don't wish to see you suffer, and I am willing to humble myself to reduce your suffering". In short, a sincere apology communicates caring, valuing, empathy, respect, validation, responsibility, an awareness and acceptance of your mistakes, remorse, an intention to change, and a wish to reconcile. When you consider that anger is a response to threat and violation, it's easy to understand how sorry can be such powerful anti-anger medicine. Sorry says "I don't wish to hurt or violate you".

There have been studies into the effects of apologies. The findings reveal that an apology is more powerful than any other forms of reconciliatory gestures. Buying flowers, paying for a cruise, offering your customers ten free orders, never repeating an offending behaviour, or bending over backwards to demonstrate remorse are all worth far less to the offended if they don't arrive with the one all-important spoken word. If you've hurt someone, saying the word sorry, and meaning it sincerely, is the only thing that's actually going to do it.

Bill Clinton made this famous apology for his sexual affair with Monika Lewinsky. "Indeed, I did have a relationship with Ms. Lewinsky that was not appropriate. In fact, it was wrong. It constituted a critical lapse in judgement and a personal failure on my part for which I am solely and completely responsible." It doesn't sound like much of an apology does it?

Saying sorry without real sincerity is probably more damaging than not saying it at all. Sorry is not a "get out of the doghouse free" card. Being sorry means being willing to accept the consequences too. Sorry may have to be delivered with genuine recompense. If you have caused loss to a customer, then a genuine apology should be accompanied with a demonstration of your sincerity in the form of compensation for the loss. If you've been selfish in your relationship, a gesture of selflessness is going to be necessary to demonstrate a desire to change, and then you need to follow up on that too. If things just revert to type once you're off the hook, you can expect resentment to return pretty quickly! Equally, if the person you're apologizing to feels like you are trying to buy their forgiveness that's going to backfire. Sorry is not a currency to be used, and neither are gifts. It needs to be from the heart, or not at all!

So here's what a real apology should look like. It should demonstrate that you understand what you've done, how and why it was hurtful, how you plan to change to ensure it doesn't happen again, and it shouldn't contain any excuses or justifications. You chose to do what you did. Don't try to justify it because that's not an apology. That sounds like you're trying to get yourself off the hook. An apology is not to ease your conscience. It is a selfless offering towards the other. If you're including yourself as a beneficiary in any way, expect to get a poor response!

Perhaps the most important thing to recognise when it comes to apologies is that there are no special requirements necessary to be able to offer them. At the most fundamental level possible, even if you have unresolved wounding, even if you're stressed, even if you're seeing things through distorted filters, it is still within your power to see that the other is hurting, and apologise. It's a choice. Refusing to say sorry is not tough. It's weak. I wholeheartedly recommend that you start thinking about your part in the continuation of any dramas which are making you angry, and ask yourself whether saying sorry might put an end to them? I can promise you that saying sorry is not as painful as you expect it to be. It will undoubtedly lead to a huge release of tension from the situation, and open the way to healing.

If offering an apology is important, then learning to receive an apology is equally important. It would be very easy to refuse someone's apology because then you get to be the one with all the power. If someone apologises to you, they metaphorically place themselves on bended knee at your feet. If you've been angry at someone for a long time there can be a strong temptation to make this moment last, or continue the drama to make them pay a bit more. Finally, you are vindicated. At last, your pain is recognised. You're the king of the castle and they are the dirty rascal. There's an important decision to be made in this moment. This person is deliberately making themselves extremely vulnerable. They are placing themselves unguarded, at your mercy. You could be tempted to milk your moment of glory, but let's understand that to do so would be both undignified and cowardly in the extreme. It's the emotional equivalent of kicking a person when they are down. Sadly, anger and rage will often do this in the World, but let's remember that the agenda here is to take actions which are not driven by anger and hatred. Milking an apology includes saying ok and then still sulking. It includes saying I forgive you, but.....and it includes a flat refusal to accept the apology. If you feel that the apology is insincere or insufficient, then it's your job to say so, and explain why. That is different from flat refusing or milking a sufficient and sincere apology. Forgiveness is not always easy, and sometimes it takes time. If you wish to accept the apology but can't find it in your heart to do so at this moment, then say so, but communicate a willingness to work towards reconciliation. Explain that you will need time to work through your feelings on the matter. If their apology is sincere, they should be willing to understand this, but never use this as a form of manipulation or power over another. It took a lot for this person to do this for you. If you take the stick they've handed to you and beat them with it, you will lose any chance of resolution. They will close down permanently, and that will be the end of it.

GRACEFUL ASSERTIVENESS

Having now considered the importance of being willing to give and receive apologies we also need to understand the importance of being able to **not** apologise for some things too! Confusing eh? Well, let's see if we can clear this up. Here's a sample list of things that you won't want to apologise for. There could be many others: -

* Being unhappy for receiving poor service from a business or service provider.

* Letting someone know that you're not okay with the way they are treating you.

* Being unable to meet unreasonable demands or expectations placed upon you.

* Saying "no" when you mean no.

* Something truly outside of your control.

As we've already explored, being in the right should never be used as a power game. That's undignified for a start, and it's also going to be ineffective as a longer-term strategy for reducing anger. You might win, but everyone will dislike you for being so merciless, and you'll be right back in a hostile World wondering why you're so angry. What goes around comes around too. If you can't be merciful, don't expect anyone to treat you nicely when the shoe is on the other foot.

Graceful assertiveness therefore includes **grace**. Assertiveness is not a tool for asserting power over others. Rather it is the tool by which we can claim our own power, and request that others honour our right to do so. We acknowledge in doing so that they have an equal right to claim their power also. Let me explain.

I believe that I have a right to refuse. In practice, I try to be as accommodating as possible, but experience has taught me where my limits are, and sometimes refusing is an act of self –preservation, not selfishness. If somebody asks something of me which I am not willing or able to deliver, it is my responsibility to myself to refuse the request. I would genuinely like to help, but my loss will outweigh their gain. It's my job to communicate my refusal in a fair and positive, but firm manner. Suppose, for instance, that I want to borrow something. There are two helpful rules about borrowing. The first is the rather cynical saying "Neither a borrower nor a lender be." Why? Well, because it's a potential recipe for disaster. There's a good chance that owner and object will not be reunited, or will be reunited with some loss to the lender (i.e it's returned in poor condition). This is a recipe for negative feelings between people, and it's a bit like doing business with friends. It's risky at best and foolhardy at worst. With that said I also learned this: "Never lend anything that you are not willing to let go of." Now this rule works better for me. I can't say that I stick to it 100% of the time. You know, you make a risk assessment and then decide, but there are some things I just won't lend to people, and the reason is simple, I'm not willing to lose that thing. Now, it's my job to communicate that gracefully. I say "I'd really love to help you out Fred, but that "*" is really important to me, and I'm afraid I just can't take the risk that something might happen to it. I know you'd look after it, but sometimes stuff happens, and I wouldn't want something like an object to ever come between us". Is this comfortable for me to say? No! Is it necessary? Yes. Now it's Fred's job to accept my message gracefully. Fred can choose how he interprets this. If he wants to, he can go away and say "What a jerk...after all the things I've done for him!" conveniently forgetting that I've loaned him loads of stuff in the past, not all of which has been returned, but I let it go. This one thing, I wasn't willing to let go of. It's about ME, not Fred. What I would hope would happen is that Fred would say to himself "Wow, that "*" must be really special. That's cool. I'd probably feel the same way about it too." No offence intended, none taken. Here's the really important part. If I went to Fred and asked to borrow something from him, I'd like it if he said yes, but I'd completely understand if he said no. Even if it was something small and seemingly inconsequential, I would still choose to respect his right to say no. I might not understand his reasoning, but I would respect his decision, with no judgement. It's just easier that way. Why should I write off a friendship or hold a grudge over an object or a favour? That's just a waste of all that is good between us. He has his reasons. That's all there is in it. No offence intended, none taken.

So, for me, that's the rules. People have a perfect right to say no, and so do I. Now, if somebody takes offence at my refusal, they might have a point, and that's for me to go away and consider. Maybe I am being unnecessarily stingy or selfish? They are allowed to express disappointment, and they are allowed to express why they are disappointed by my refusal, but they are not allowed to be hostile or violent towards me. If, after consideration, I am still unwilling to agree to their request, I can tell them why in an assertive but graceful way. And there it should end. If someone then decides to hold my refusal against me, I would now consider the problem to be theirs, not mine. They are not angry because I have harmed them. They are angry because they are choosing to interpret my refusal personally. I'm not doing that **to** them. They are doing that to themselves! So that's why I won't apologise for saying no when I mean no. Should I be angry with them for being angry with me? It would be much better to have further calm dialogue using a nonviolent communication format.

So, here is the format you use when being assertive. It's simple, and highly effective: -

* State the facts. Do not blame. Just say what is.

* Explain how it makes you feel.

* Explain "why" it makes you feel that way.

* Ask for help in resolving the situation, and/or suggest a way to resolve it.

Here's what I'm going to say to Fred. "Fred. It appears that I have offended you with my refusal to loan you my car. I'm saddened to think that I have upset you, and I feel that you may have misunderstood my motivations. The reason I'm sad is that we've been friends for a long time, and I really care about you. The reason I'm not loaning my car to you is that I have a rule. That rule is that I don't loan anything to anyone which I'm not willing to let go of. It's not personal. I apply that rule to everyone in my life, and I'm afraid my car falls into the category of things I'm not willing to let go of. I'm sure you would look after it, but sometimes things happen which are outside of our control. I'd really like you to not feel sore about this. I wouldn't want such a small thing to come between us. Do you think you could accept my decision without being angry?"

Note that I have not attacked Fred in any way. Neither have I apologised. I have owned the decision, and explained why I feel the way I do, and asked Fred to help me. He is perfectly entitled to tell me he can't get over it. That's valid too, but that still leaves it being Fred's problem, not mine. I'll have to tell him "I'll be still here as your Friend Fred, there's no hard feelings on my part". It works both ways. I'm not being a power tripper here. It is my way or the highway, but it's an act of self-preservation, not an act of hostility. If our friendship survives this, Fred will know that I'm not willing to loan him my car, but he should know by now that I'll come over and do his garden with him any time because I do it all the time. He helps me with the computer. That's what our friendship is based on. He just needs to let it go. If he wants to throw our friendship away because he can't, then that is something I have no control over.

This is what assertiveness is.

CHAPTER EIGHT – WHY BOTHER?

Let's pretend that in a perfect World you will now have changed your life circumstances, reduced your overall stress levels, resolved your historical wounding, made some changes in the language that you use when describing events to yourself, cleaned your muddy filters, given up on trying to control everything, reduced your expectation levels, recognised that softness controls hardness, ditched the sarcasm and veiled attacks, learned to consider that criticism could be constructive, decided to look for what might be right in situations, see the best in people, extend trust, communicate your true feelings to your loved ones, learned to listen to theirs, let the rest of the World know what your terms of business are, learned that humble pie tastes better than losing everything, and now understand why sorry is so vitally important to give and receive. Phew! That's quite a lot to take on board isn't it? Should you expect yourself to have it all pinned down because you read a book? No. My work is about giving people the understanding and the tools necessary to get to grips, in a down to Earth way, with what's causing the difficulty. That doesn't mean that the work is done. In fact, this is probably just the beginning of your journey. It's not possible to cover every eventuality in the pages of a book like this. I do recognise that the examples given are beautifully neat and tidy, and in real life, things are often more complicated. I'd like to share another tale from my own life to illustrate this point.

My grandparents owned a house. They had lived in this house since 1947, and had been good friends with their immediate neighbour. My grandfather and the neighbour had made a joint agreement to knock out the wall between their front gardens and create a shared driveway which they could both use to park their cars. This was a peaceful arrangement for decades. The neighbour died, and a new family moved in. My grandmother didn't drive, so when my grandfather died, she didn't use the driveway any more, other than for guests. Fast forward many years. My grandmother became ill with dementia and was hospitalised, and eventually she went to a care home. I was charged with the responsibility of selling her house to pay the eight hundred pounds a week care home fees. When I went to sell the house, the new neighbour claimed that he owned a larger part of the driveway than he did, which made it technically impossible to park a car should any new buyers wish to do so. I explained the situation, and pleaded with the neighbour to be reasonable, but he refused, explaining that he was in debt, and couldn't afford to reduce his "investment". At the time, the housing market was in a slump and the outcome was that nobody would buy a house with a dispute. He made it literally impossible for me to sell the house because there was now an officially noted "boundary dispute", and nobody but Monty Python would want to buy an argument! I sought legal advice and discovered that despite having photographs of the original positioning of the walls, I would still have to fight a long court battle, which could cost more than the value of the house itself. All the while I was receiving invoices for over three thousand pounds per month from the care home. It was eventually resolved because an investor came in and bought both my grandparents' house and the neighbours' house and re-structured the whole thing, but it was two years of hell, all incidentally a hundred and sixty miles away from my own home. As you can imagine, it was hugely stressful, and I was pretty furious. Not only was he wrong, and I had the pictures and deeds which proved it, but he was making my life a living hell deliberately, and for no discernible gain. In this instance, common sense and diplomacy didn't work. I will admit that murder did cross my mind! In addition to this, I had spent four months of my life driving the three hundred plus miles round trip every weekend without fail to visit my Grandmother, and then spent every available hour renovating the house to make it sale ready. Just as it was completed I received a phone call from the neighbour. The house was flooded. A pipe had split in the loft in the freezing weather. The house was literally gutted. The ceilings collapsed, the concrete floors were soaked through and the plaster fell off the walls. It was left a soggy shell. It cost over thirty thousand pounds and many months to dry and restore the property. Then there was a year-long battle with the insurance company for payment. Despite agreeing to pay the claim, they just didn't! They consistently ignored my phone calls and letters. They deliberately delayed paying out until I was literally employing my own solicitor to take them to court for non-payment. Meanwhile I was receiving legal summons from the restorers as I had no money to pay them for their work until the insurers paid me. There were many more factors including poor healthcare for my Nan, family in-fighting, and a complete lack of time and finance. I was also being a full time therapist! It was a bad few years!

Please do know then that I recognise that there are situations which can cause your blood to boil which really have little to do with your handling of something, and everything to do with the situation itself. Being truly powerless is not a nice experience. I'd also guess that common sense means that you already know that. All we can do with something like this is have great patience, and keep pushing for a resolution. These types of situations will challenge a Saint.

Nonetheless, the **principles** are what are being communicated, and for the most part life is not as intense or impossible as the situation I described above. These are the necessary tools and now you'll need to master them. You'll need to be innovative, and experimental, but you now have the equipment you need.

BRINGING IT ALL TOGETHER

Beyond the occasional unavoidable impossible situations, I want to encourage you to recognise that you have many rights as a human being, and that it is your job to claim these for yourself. This book's subtitle was originally "Temper Management In An Unsympathetic World". While I've stopped well short of mollycoddling my readers here, that spirit still stands.

Angry people are generally not bad people, and all the while the World keeps pointing judgemental fingers, there will simply be more reason to remain disconnected and angry. Central to this book's message is the principle that you do need to take personal responsibility for your anger, but you should not blame yourself for it. You didn't ask to be angry. If things had been different, you wouldn't have been. Chronic anger is the result of many different factors, most of which you had little or no say in when they were occurring. Still, it has been your lot in life up to this point, and I hope that I have deconstructed any arguments your mind may have been selling you with regards to remaining angry. It needs to become a non-option going forwards.

There's an important point here. I have, I hope, illustrated the mechanisms and reasons for anger, as well as highlighted why anger can be a powerful temptress too. Do keep in mind that nobody but yourself can actually make the decision to quit being angry. Even when you have made the decision, one of the central obstacles you'll be faced with is the urge to stay angry. It's just easier. This will be more pronounced if you're also anxious, depressed, or just plain exhausted. Your emotions may still run high, but here's the point. You're going to need to get past that. You'll need to push through these feelings with every bit of reason you can muster because much as anger will tell you it's your friend, you have to know that it's not. At least not the chronic anger you arrived at this book seeking to resolve. This kind of anger will give you cheap shots of temporary power that will leave you with a whole load of nothing in return. I'd like to encourage you to remember that there are almost certainly people in your life who care deeply for you, and if you need a reason to do this, then do it for them too. I do not want to lecture you. I'm sure you've had all the lecturing you can stand from others and yourself. All I want to do is to encourage you to do what needs to be done, and to mark it up as important enough to bother with. Many times I've read a book and thought "Yes. That makes sense", and then gone back to doing my life exactly how I always did it. Then I wondered why I still felt bad a year later. These things don't go away. You really don't want to wait until it really is too late and you've spent another year of your life not enjoying it, only to find that you've done irreparable damage to the things or people you cherish the most. Even if you have people around you who will put up with your "ways" you have to ask yourself whether they should have to. Please don't delay. It's possible to cool it! The only question now, is will you?

Please remember that tough as this talk may be, I remain on your side. I'm passionate because I know that things could be better for you. I also have an ulterior motive. I want to live in a World that's less hostile. I recognise that every human being who reduces their anger is one step closer to that World.

You do have work ahead of you, and I'd suggest that you are patient with yourself as you put this new understanding into practice in your life. Don't underestimate the size of the undertaking. It won't happen overnight, but by claiming your true power, knowing your rights, and having clarity about how to protect yourself in an empowered way against perceived attacks, you will have less reason to be angry than ever before. The tools are in this book. If you haven't done the exercises as you've been reading then as suggested earlier, please revisit the information, and try actually using the exercises. Remember that if you really can't get past something personal, there are plenty of great therapists out there who can help you. It won't cost you the Earth, and they are generally very grown up beings who won't judge you, or make you feel silly for asking for help. You may find it hard to believe, but even though I don't know you, I do care about what happens to you. I would like to see a World where everyone suffers less. This isn't simple idealism. It comes from a place of suffering. I have suffered terribly in my life. I'd like to think that my work can save others from a similar fate. It's that simple really.

PHILOSOPHICAL THOUGHTS

It's a tough World out there. I feel some anger most days about the continued injustice, corruption, double standards, lack of empathy, selfishness, greed, hostility, and ignorance we all find in evidence when we look around us. I'm also aware that the World is incredibly complex, and there are no easy solutions to the World's problems. While there may be tiny sparks of creativity and genius which fly out from the centre and change the World in some surprising and profound way, for the rest of us we can only hope to have some beneficial effect upon our own very local universe. I have lived more than half my life now. I am aware that I will not be here forever. As the Zen Master said "The problem with you is you think you have time!" We don't. We have now, and that's it. Everything else is uncertain. The choices we make today matter. I believe that our local universe matters greatly because it is not only space which is affected by your way of being, but also time.

Sadly, wounding is passed down from generation to generation. If you've been really angry in life, there's a good chance that's because you've been given reason to be. If your parents were angry, and treated you badly as a result, there's a good chance that their parents were wounded too. On it goes. The future is dependent on healing. If we continue to pass our wounding on to our children, the negative effects of that will ripple out into space and time, possibly for many generations to come. Somebody somewhere is going to need to make a heroic effort to break the cycle. It might as well be you. Consider that healing the anger in your being will create positive ripples not only into your local space, but also potentially far into the future too. I know that there's a surge of anti-sentimentalism in the World right now. I recognise that there are people waiting to tear down these lovey-dovey ideals of healing and harmony; to say that they are unrealistic and childish. I don't accept that. Those perspectives are angry too.

As I hope I have demonstrated in this book, uncontrolled anger and hatred are illogical positions. They do nothing but harm. The Human Race still has the potential to become a thing of incredible beauty. It's not someone else's job to make that happen. It's ours. It won't happen in our lifetimes, but we are all links in a chain stretching from the beginning of our species to our destination, and what we contribute today will make a difference tomorrow. If you can help those around you to recognise the dangers of hatred and the pleasures of peace, by healing your own wounds and becoming a calm and warm person in the World, then you will leave a legacy to be proud of because that will surely continue to flow outwards like ripples on a lake. Your children will grow up in an atmosphere of peacefulness and support. Your colleagues will like having you around. Your partner will enjoy being with you. Your friends will want to spend time with you, and you may achieve great things. More important than all of this though is one simple fact. You will have a life which you actually enjoy.

I sincerely hope that this offering will have helped you to step into a more peaceful way of being that will make your life and those lives around you a much brighter place to be. Thank You for reading! I send you my very best wishes for the journey ahead.

Over and out!

One Last Thing

If you enjoyed this book, and better still if it has helped you I'd be eternally grateful if you would leave a review at Amazon to let others know it was a positive read for you! We independent authors rely heavily on positive reviews to gain visibility within the Amazon store so believe me when I say that every single one posted is noted with huge thanks!

Here is the link to leave your review: -

UK: - https://www.amazon.co.uk/dp/B01HENG6LW

USA: - https://www.amazon.com/dp/B01HENG6LW

And, finally, I'd love to stay connected. Please do come over and join me on my Facebook page at

www.facebook.com/stressanxietydepression

You can also sign up for my newsletter and grab your free gifts at

www.youcanfixyouranxiety.com

I'll keep you updated with news, free stuff, offers, events, and of course notice of new releases with special offers for newsletter subscribers! There are more books on their way.

This book is available in Paperback and Ebook (Kindle) format from Amazon.

Thank you for supporting my work!

Is stress, anxiety, or depression ruining your life? Do you believe that there are no answers? Are those "quick fix" approaches failing to deliver results?

That may well be because you're much more like a garden than you are an electrical appliance! Healing anxiety is an organic process, not just nuts and bolts!

* Please note. This book was previously released under the title "You Can Fix Your Anxiety"*

Anxiety Relief is a warm, compassionate, and expert book to help anxious, panicky, or stressed people, written from both sides of the therapeutic couch!

If you're suffering, and you don't know how to gain relief from your anxiety, then this book is for you. It's wide in scope but laser-focussed on ensuring that you get results! The tools and understanding presented here are the same proven tools that John has been using to help anxious people successfully recover for many years.

Inside "Anxiety Relief" you'll discover:-

- How to create the correct mindset for full and permanent recovery from (even severe) anxiety.
- How to fully understand the brain's evolutionary role in creating stress, anxiety, depression, panic and negative thinking, and how to use that understanding to take back control.
- Why self-love, the right resources, and appropriate skills are **essential** components for recovery when anxiety attacks!
- Why just throwing random "techniques" at an anxiety problem won't resolve the core of the problem, and what to do instead.
- How compassionate connection with your most vulnerable self will turbo-charge your recovery time and offer long-term stability, and how to do it!
- Why your subconscious mind keeps you locked in anxiety, and how to work WITH that mind to **stop** the internal war!
- How to avoid soul-destroying, resource-sucking wrong turns!
- And much, much more!

Anxiety Relief is written with sparkling clarity to provide an expert step by step anxiety recovery system which any anxiety sufferer can understand and put into immediate use. This book goes well beyond the usual "Do this and you'll feel better" formula however. It will provide you with an explanation of the many angles you can employ to make things better and provide you with the great missing ingredient that causes many anxiety sufferers to fail in recovery – HEART!

If that sounds mysterious to you, then there's almost certainly something here that you've overlooked before.

This book offers you the tools and understanding that will reach deep enough to finally make the real difference!

Buy "Anxiety Relief" today to let this powerful, practical, <u>sincere</u> book from a true "anxiety insider" show you how

to reach to the HEART of your anxiety, and find your easy smile again!

You can find this book at these links: -

UK: https://www.amazon.co.uk/dp/B01EAZN8HM

USA: https://www.amazon.com/dp/B077X2NWFJ

You can also go the website at www.youcanfixyouranxiety.com if you'd like to learn more about the books (for a full list) or contact me directly on john@hypnotherapyforlife.co.uk

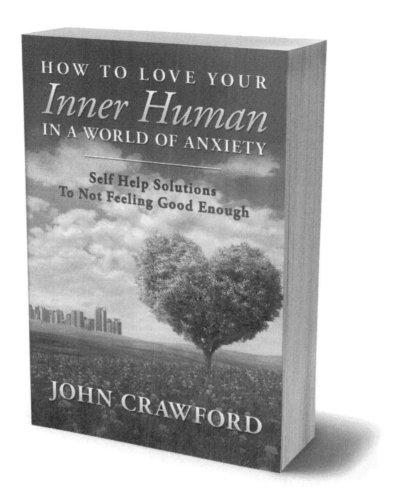

New for 2019!

Who's got your back? You do! Self-love is not a luxury item. It's an absolutely essential part of happiness and confidence in a challenging world. If you don't feel good enough, or just want to feel more at ease within yourself, then this book is for you.

In a world obsessed with vanity, performance, status, and possessions, the pressure to measure up is making us unhappy and anxious. This book is an antidote to that anxiety.

In an illuminating journey of self-empowerment, John takes us from the stone-age to the stars, and from flawed to just fine. He demonstrates along the way how we can recover our lost power, forgive ourselves deeply, learn acceptance of our imperfections, and become our own best friend and ally for the rest of our lives.

This powerful, joyful book will guide you well beyond the standard "be kind to yourself" advice. It will provide you with unique heart-and-mind transforming tools to completely redefine your relationship with yourself, and the world - at the very deepest level.

When nobody else knows what you're going through, there's only one person who can truly be by your side – and that's you. We cannot afford to leave this most important relationship to chance.

If you're ready to make peace with your past, silence the world's judgements, own your voice, and protect yourself with fierce love, then you'll find what you're looking for in these pages.

You may have been waiting a lifetime for this book. Grab your copy today because your inner human will thank you, and life is too short to not have your best friend by your side!

How To Love Your Inner Human – Amazon UK -
https://www.amazon.co.uk/dp/B07M6Z778N

How To Love Your Inner Human – Amazon USA -
https://www.amazon.com/dp/B07M6Z778N

And don't forget (as on page 3) that you can download your free copy of my third book "Dear Anxiety. This Is My Life", which details my own personal journey of recovery from severe anxiety, plus two more professionally recorded anti-anxiety recordings here: -

https://goo.gl/A3MQoi

About John Crawford

John Crawford is truly qualified to share expertise on how to overcome anger, anxiety, OCD, and depression. Not only has he been a professional therapist for more than thirteen years, he was himself held hostage by severe anxiety and depression for many years in his twenties. His understanding of the field is therefore more than purely intellectual. It's deeply personal and committed.

John ran his own thriving business as a one to one hypnotherapist/psychotherapist specialising in the treatment of anxiety, depression, and OCD, from 2003-2016. He quickly gained a solid professional reputation in the Bristol and Bath area of the UK for anxiety-related difficulties. He has over seven thousand hours of clinical experience in helping people to overcome their emotional and mental health challenges.

He is a significant contributor of sections of the training materials used by Clifton Practice Hypnotherapy Training (CPHT), a now international Hypnotherapy Training Centre with twelve branches in the United Kingdom. CPHT is recognised for its outstanding Solution-Focussed Brief Therapy training.

John has spoken professionally for the Association for Professional Hypnosis and Psychotherapy, Clifton Practice Hypnotherapy Training, OCD Action (the largest national OCD charity in the UK), as well as regularly at smaller supervisory events for local practitioners. He has also written for the highly respected online anxiety sufferers' resource, No More Panic. He was a registered and accredited member of three leading therapeutic organisations - Association for Professional Hypnosis & Psychotherapy, National Hypnotherapy Society, and National Council of Psychotherapists, up until 2016 when he closed his one to one practice to focus on writing and teaching. His main qualifications include:-

Diploma in Hypnotherapy and Psychotherapy - Clifton Practice Training (formerly EICH)

Hypnotherapy Practitioner Diploma - National externally (NCFE) accredited to NVQ 4.

Diploma in Cognitive Behavioural Hypnotherapy - Externally (NCFE) accredited to NVQ4.

Anxiety Disorders Specialist Certification - The Minnesota Institute of Advanced Communication Skills.

He lives happily in Bristol (UK) with his wife and cat, and produces music in his spare time.

Printed in Great
Britain
by Amazon